THE HISTORY OF PSYCHOLOGY

THE CONTRIBUTIONS OF 100 HISTORICAL FIGURES

SCIENCE INSPIRES. SCIENCE DIRECTS.
SCIENCE CONNECTS.

Allan G. Hedberg, Ph.D.

Clinical Psychologist

ISBN: 979-8-89465-030-2 (sc)
ISBN: 979-8-89465-031-9 (e)

Printed in the United States of America.

Integrity Publishing
39343 Harbor Hills Blvd Lady Lake,
FL 32159

www.integrity-publishing.com

CONTENTS

PSYCHOLOGY'S MAJOR ACHIEVEMENTS

APPENDIX

PERSPECTIVE

The righteous need no tombstones.

Their words are their monuments.

TALMUD, Persahim, 119a

Dr. Hippocrates

Do No Harm Avenue

Island of Cos, Greece Summer, 380 B.C.E

Dear Modern Day "Physician:"

I am often asked the question, What is good health? Let me answer it. To me, good health results from the proper balance of body fluids, while poor health comes from the imbalance of our body fluids. Essentially, it is a result of proper living to which the body responds favorably. Unlike my ancestors, I believe in mental functions as the work of God or demons, but I constantly seek naturalistic answers.

I was born in 460 B.C. I am soon to die. I am considered the founder of medicine. My father was a physician in his day. I studied and practiced here on the Greek island of Cos. I treated individuals who were disabled and who came to the island for the hot springs.

I divorce medicine from religion and superstition. I maintain that all diseases, rather than being the work of the gods, have natural causes. I believe and teach that most of the physical and mental ills of the patient had a biochemical basis. I base this explanation of health and illness on the prevailing theories of matter, water, fire and air.

Further, I believe good health is the result of the proper balance of the four body fluids, which corresponded to the four elements: blood corresponded with fire, phlegm with water, black bile with earth, and yellow bile with air.

Hence, for years to come, physicians will attribute many illnesses to hormonal imbalances. They will try to cure it by draining off excess humor, called the procedure of bloodletting, or by administering medicine and thereby supplying one that is lacking in the body's makeup Unfortunately, this approach will cause significant harm, particularly the use of bloodletting. I also use this same theory to explain mental health and illness. I believe that if the four humors are in proper balance, consciousness and thought will function well, but if any of the humors are either in excess or in short supply, mental illness of one kind or another will result. From this beginning, other philosophers and scientists will come along and further develop the concept that personality differences and traits are humor-based.

From these humble beginnings, we will come to better understand the body, the mind, and the soul of man.

The very best solution to both physical and mental diseases appear to be the use of tonic water. Some call it mineral water or Salzer water. It serves to balance the body's fluids and restore health. You will see more use of it in years to come. It may even come in different flavors to make it more palatable and easier on the stomach.

The best to you all as you further develops a more comprehensive understanding of the body and mind.

One last word: "Above all, do no harm." I wish you well.

Respectfully,

Hippocrates

PREFACE

I suspect no one wants to be famous. How about being rich? Probably! Probably not! Throughout history, psychologists have worked diligently and sacrificially. Becoming famous was not their passion or desire. It happened because of their diligent efforts to study and understand a portion of the human mind and explain why man does what he does. Fame and riches were not their pursuits. However, it was bestowed upon them due to their devoted studies, writings, research, and teachings.

Below are twelve characteristics of famous therapists that emerged from my review of their writings. They all fit a pattern. The pattern is admirable. The pattern sets an example for all of us, no matter what our field of study. The pattern that emerges is to work hard, share with others, build a circle of mentors, teach others, be an example, and address important life issues, to name a few. To be sure, people do not set out to be famous; it is bestowed upon them due to their years of dedicated studies, writings, and teaching. A famous identity is a result of challenging work; it is not what drives hard work.

We need famous people around us. They teach us how to live our lives. They encourage us, stimulate innovative ideas, give us directions, and create hope that we can do likewise.

The history of these famous therapists is vital to our future as a profession and to every individual therapist serving our communities diligently every day. When serving a community, it is necessary to have the guidance of strong mentors and exemplary forefathers. Some of the benefits of studying strong therapists of the past include inspiration, connection, direction, and focused attention on our own service to a community and patient population.

To be sure, we all gain strength from the lives and professional practices of successful men and women and the lives they model. In this book, we will take a journey back into history, peer into the lives of a host of psychological scientists and therapists, and learn how they dealt with challenges both personally and professionally. Most importantly, we will learn from the lives and works of a selected historical array of heroes, leaders, and scholars.

Let's all move forward together as scholars, researchers, authors, and pursuers of historical and scientific truth. So, we all can make our own mark on the flow of a psychological theme for a better world ahead.

Lastly, how does one organize a book on the history of any subject? I chose from among the options to do it chronologically by the birth date of each historical figure selected for the book. This organizational structure gives us an overview of the sequential unfolding of the science of psychology and the distinctive touch of each contributor. Each one built on the work of those who went on before and advanced psychology as a science, one step at a time, on experiment or study at a time.

The book is a product of my three classes and personal reading on the history and systems of psychology. It is also a result of lectures I attended, site visits to historical places, discussions with colleagues, and the reading of several books on the history of psychology and of several historical figures. Sometimes I leaned heavily on certain sources, perhaps too much, but I did so in the interest of bringing psychology to the reader. I am a better psychologist today because of this writing project. I hope you will also be better in your field of study and work because of your reading of this book.

Allan G. Hedberg, Ph.D.

THE HISTORICAL UNFOLDING OF PSYCHOLOGY

Psychology is defined as "the scientific study of behavior and mental processes." Others have defined it as "the study of human behavior." More generally, it is "the study of why man does what he does."

History records 1653 as the year of the first Ph.D. degree, although there are roots of such a degree dating back to the middle ages. The first MD degree can be traced back to 1703. In comparison, the Ph.D. degree has stood strong as the first doctorate degree in the field of the "healing arts." Further, the Ph.D. has a stronger history and pattern of research, teaching, scientific studies, and the healing arts than medicine. Psychology as a profession and scientific study was one of the first recognized fields of study. It was in 1854, in Leipzig, Germany, that Gustav Fechner created the first psychological theory of how judgments about sensory experiences are made and how to experiment on them. To be sure, psychological theory and findings came into full bloom. It is no longer primitive. It was during these years that psychology became recognized for its own field of study and methodology. It was increasingly acknowledged as an independent area of study from medicine, psychiatry, neurology, and philosophy.

Shortly afterwards, in 1879, Wilhelm Wundt founded in Leipzig, Germany, the first psychological laboratory dedicated exclusively to psychological research. Wundt was also the first person to refer to himself as a *psychologist.* A notable precursor of Wundt was Ferdinand Ueberwasser (1752-1812), who designated himself *Professor of Empirical Psychology and Logic* in 1783 and gave lectures on empirical psychology at the Old University of Münster, Germany.

Soon thereafter, various kinds of applied psychology appeared. G. Stanley Hall brought scientific pedagogy to the United States from Germany in the early 1880s. John Dewey's educational theory of the 1890s was another example. In the 1890s, Hugo Münsterberg began writing about the application of psychology to industry, law, and other fields. Lightner Witmer established the first psychological clinic in the 1890s. James McKeen Cattell adapted Francis Galton's anthropometric methods to generate the first program of mental testing in the 1890s. In Vienna, meanwhile, Sigmund Freud developed an independent approach to the study of the mind called psychoanalysis.

John B. Watson created behaviorism in the 20th century, and B. F. Skinner advanced it. Behaviorism emphasized the study of overt behavior because that could be quantified and easily measured. Early behaviorists considered the study of the "mind" too vague for productive scientific study.

The final decades of the 20th century saw the rise of cognitive science, an interdisciplinary approach to studying the human mind. Cognitive science again considers the "mind" as a subject for investigation, using the tools of cognitive psychology, linguistics, computer science, philosophy, behaviorism, and neurobiology. This form of investigation has proposed that a wide understanding of the human mind is possible and that such an understanding may be applied to other research domains, such as artificial intelligence.

Indeed, psychology, as in every developing science, has much application to many areas of daily life and effective and positive living. For example, the field of neuropsychology is a rapidly growing field of study with much potential for learning new ways we process information and form behavior patterns. Indeed, it will be the field of study in the next decade that will be life-shaping.

Adopted from Wikipedia

THE CHRONOLOICAL HISTORY OF PSYCHOLOGY'S MAJOR ACHIEVEMENTS

Ancient History: Overview

c. 1500 BCE: Clinical depression first noted . . . Egyptian manuscript

c. 1000 BCE: Emotions and physical responses are noted and dubbed "physiological psychology." . . . Avicenna

c. 460 BCE: Personality depends on the levels of four humors in the body. . . Hippocrates

c. 325 BCE: The four sources of happiness are identified. . . Aristotle

c. 190 BCE: The four types of personality were identified based on body humors. . . Claudius Galen

Early History: Overview

1628: The body and soul are separate. . . Rene Descartes

1653: The first Ph.D. degree conferred, primarily for teaching purposes

1758: The "Treatise on Madness" is published. . . Battie

1783: For the first-time, psychology as a profession was recognized in the academic world.

1791: The first of over 100 reports of Multiple Personality Disorder. . . Eberhardt Gmelin

1810: The introduction of Phrenology as a way to study the individualistic characteristics of man, and determine why he does what he does

1813: Psychological concepts and research findings are first applied to the work situation, and the birth of industrial psychology. . . Hugo Munsterberg

1816: The mind is dynamic with a conscious and unconscious component . . . Johann F. Herbart

1819: The technique of hypnosis is introduced. . . Abbe Faria

1843: Hypnosis is defined as a high degree of concentration on a single idea, resulting is heightened suggestibility. . . James Braid

1844: The publication of the Statistical Classification of Institutionalized Patients, which was considered the forerunner to the Diagnostic and Statistical Manual.

1844: The establishment of the American Psychiatric Association

1854: Signal Detection Theory was first formulated. . . Gustav Fechner

1859: All traits are inherited. . . Charles Darwin

1861: The area of the brain responsible for speech was identified as the Broca area. . . Paul Broca

1869: Nature is more important than nurture. . . Francis Galton

1874: Damage to any area of the brain causes the loss of specific skills. . . Carl Wernicke

1871: Intellectual abilities are inherited. . . Charles Darwin

1876: Familiarity increases positive feelings, but oversaturation breeds aversion. . . Gustav Fechner

1879: The first psychology laboratory was founded in Leipzig, Germany. . . Wilhelm Wundt

1880: Through the use of hypnosis, we came to study suggestibility, conformity, and social Influence. . . Hippolyte Bernheim

1884: Individual differences became a focus area of study. . . Francis Galton

1885: Memory functions and the "forgetting curve" were first identified. . . Hermann Ebbinghaus

1886: Freud begins to offer therapy to patients in Vienna, Austria. . . Freud

1887: The first journal in psychology was published. . . G. Stanley Hall

1889: States of hysteria and dissociation were considered to be the basis for splitting the Personality. . . Pierre Janet

1891: The establishment of the American Psychological Association

1895: The first laboratory in psychodiagnostics opened. . . Alfred Binet

1896: The first psychology clinic opened in America for treating patients. . . Witmer

1898: We repeat those responses that lead to satisfying effects. . . Edward Thorndike

Modern History: Overview

1905: The first intelligence test was designed and used widely. . . Alfred Binet

1905: First woman elected president of the American Psychological Association. . . Calkins

1912: Published Experimental Studies of the Perception of Movement. . . Wertheimer

1913: Behaviorism introduced and the conditioned emotional response. . . John B. Watson

1915: The theory of psychosexual development was introduced. . . Sigmund Freud

1917: Man is a social animal. . . John Dewey

1918: The experiments of "Little Albert" applied to the conditioning of babies. . . John B. Watson

1920: Intelligence is considered to be genetic. . . Cyril Burt

1920: The study of fear based on "Little Albert" was published. . . Rayner

1921: The personality traits of introversion and extraversion are introduced. . . Carl Jung

1924: John Watson leaves the field of psychology in disgrace and enters the field of advertising and works on a project to get the public to accept women smoking. . . John B. Watson

1926: The key characteristics of geniuses are tremendous persistence and motivation. . . Catharine Cox

1927: Classical conditioning was identified as a learning process. . . Ivan Pavlov

1929: Learning involves the whole brain. . . Karl Lashley

1930: Learning occurs through the process of "operant conditioning." . . . B.F. Skinner

1935: "Imprinting" was identified as a new learning process at critical times in life. . . Konrad Lorenz

1938: Learning can occur after only one exposure; repetition is not necessary. . . Edwin G. Guthrie

1940: The publication of the Minnesota Multiphasic Personality Inventory. . . Hathaway, McKinley, and Butcher

1941: Freud faced his major opponent, which led to the establishment of the American Institute of Psychoanalysis. . . Karen Horney

1942: Client-centered therapy was introduced. . . Carl Rogers

1943: True reinforcement occurs when a basic human need is satisfied. . . Clark L. Hall

1946: Finding meaning in all aspects of life, especially suffering, is necessary. . . Viktor Frankl

1947: The three-factor model of personality was developed. . . Hans Eysenck

1948: Cognitive maps are developed as we go about our daily business. . . Edward Tolman

1949: The learning process involves the connecting of neurons called "Cell Assemblies." . . . Donald Hebb

1950: The seven stages of psychosocial development were introduced. . . Eric Eerikson

1951: People will conform and override their own judgment to do so. . . Solomon Asch

1953: The first edition of the Diagnostic and Statistical Manual was published. . . American Psychiatric Association

1954: The ideal of self- actualization is identified. . . Abraham Maslow

1955: The idea of a "death instinct" is proposed. . . Melanie Klein

1956: The human brain is limited to seven chunks of information. . . George A. Miller

1957: A person's speech develops from one's behavioral and genetic history. . . B.F. Skinner

1958: Systematic desensitization is introduced as a treatment of choice for neurosis and anxiety. . . Joseph Wolpe

1959: Cognitive psychology is formulated. . . Norm Chomsky

1960: Bio-feedback techniques are introduced for psycho-physiolo gically based Disorders. . . Neil Miller

1961: Rational thinking was put forth as a critical part of healthy living. . . Albert Ellis

1962: The highly controversial experiments on obedience involving high levels of electric shocks were undertaken at Yale. . . Stanley Milgram

1963: People will override their own moral values to obey authority. . . Stanley Milgram

1963: The concept of observational learning is introduced. . . Bandura

1964: Family therapy was introduced as the treatment of choice for family-based problems. . . Virginia Satir

1964: The Three Christ's of Ypsilani. . . Milton Rokeach

1965: Choice theory was introduced, which helps a person live within reality. . . William Glasser

1966: The mental health community-based service system began to take shape in many states, starting with Minnesota. . . Herb Dorken

1967: Cognitive Behavioral Therapy is the treatment of choice for depression. . . Aaron Beck

1968: Personality is not the basis of our behavior; situations and context play a major role . . . Walter Mischel

1969: The first graduate school offering an applied degree in psychology, the Psy.D. Degree. . . The University of Illinois, Baylor University, and the California School of Professional Psychology. . . Nick Cummings and others

1970: Controlled drinking by alcoholics became a focus of research, with mixed results. . . McDonald, Hedberg, and Campbell

1971: The "jigsaw" classroom was used to reduce ethical rivalry and encourage desegregated classrooms. . . Elliot Aronson

1972: Gender-related research commenced, the competent woman studies. . . Janet Taylor Spence

1973: The psychiatric notion of sane and insane was challenged. . . David Rosenhan

1974: Gender differences were a subject of much study. . . Eleanor E. Maccoby

1975: California was the leading state in the use of electro-convulsive shock treatment.

1977: Consciousness can be split up by hypnosis. . . Ernest Hilgard

1978: Memory and the retrieval of information are mood-dependent. . . Gordon H. Bower

1979: Eyewitness memory is fallible and may be used with caution in courtroom testimony. . . Elizabeth Lotfus

1980: Brain imaging techniques to map the brain were developed. . . Several researchers

1990: The formulation of the "big five" personality traits: openness, neuroticism, agreeableness, conscientiousness, and extraversion. . . Several researchers

1991: The study of how the mind senses reality. . . Jerome Bruner

1991: The theory on how children acquire language published. . . Steven Pinker

1993: The subjective Rorschach test of inkblots is finally objectified. . . John Exner

1995: Growing up with autism became a focus of study. . . Simon Baron-Cohen

1996: The study of stress and its effects on human behavior became a focus of much research. . . S. Folkman and others

2000: Cognitive therapy became the standard treatment for anxiety, panic disorders, and OCD disorders. . . Paul Salkovskis and others

2002: The concept of the Blank Slate was introduced. . . Steven Pinker

2003: Behavior reveals personality; personality does not predict behavior. . . Walter Mischel

2004: The three motivational components of job performance applied to leadership. . . Daniel Goldman

2006: Emotions are distinctly different from feelings, and they follow rules. . . Nico Frijda

2008: The psychiatric enterprise was challenged and questioned for its validity. . . Thomas Szaez

2009: The study of geniuses linked it to genetics and good surroundings... Dean Keith Simonton

2014: The Nobel Peace Prize for the discovery of the cells that facilitate memory and navigation. . . O'Keefe, Moser, and Moser

2016: Major papers written on transgender children, morality, empathy, Trump culture, bilinguals, and prejudice. . . Annual Review, 2016

2020: The relationship between social media, gaming, and violence is examined. . . C. J. Ferguson

2021: The development and future use of artificial intelligence in psychology. . . Hull, Malgaroli, Fiske, and Luxton

2022: Publication of Pioneers of Psychology. . . Fancher and Rutherford

2023: The use of Facebook and other media to help parents deal with social media with their children. . . Prinstein, Sellers, Davis, and others

2024: It is anticipated that we will see much psychological research in the fields of neurology, artificial intelligence, mental health prevention, coaching, justice and criminal reform, to name a few.

THE FORMATION OF THE AMERICAN PSYCHOLOGICAL ASSOCIATION

It all began humbly enough. In 1892, Granville Stanley Hall, professor of psychology and president of Clark University, invited 26 American psychologists to join him in forming a psychological association. A dozen invitees attended the first organizational meeting in Hall's office on July 8, 1892. There, they founded the American Psychological Association. The participants learned that many psychologists who could not attend the meeting, such as John Dewey and Lightner Witmer, had agreed to join, and they selected two psychologists who had not been originally invited, Hugo Münsterberg of Harvard and Edward Titchener of Cornell. They elected Hall as the first president and scheduled their first meeting at the University of Pennsylvania for December of that year.

Hall, a student of William James, had founded the first American laboratory and Ph.D. program in psychology at Johns Hopkins University in 1883. He also began the *American Journal of Psychology*, the first American psychology journal, that same year. When Hall founded the APA as an association committed to "the advancement of psychology as a science" (although this goal was not officially established until 1906), he also conceived it as an institutional means of promoting relations with other professional organizations to which psychologists could usefully contribute. Hall and many of his colleagues and students also promoted psychology as the scientific grounding of pedagogy.

From its inception, membership in the APA was inclusive, at least with respect to religion and gender. The charter members included Edward Pace, a Catholic, and Joseph Jastrow, a Jew, who devised conventions for reporting that evolved into APA style. Two women, Mary Calkins and Christine Ladd-Franklin, were elected members in 1893.

But membership did not guarantee equal standing. Calkins studied at Harvard under James and Münsterberg, who judged her dissertation on learned paired associates to be the best produced in the Department of Philosophy. Yet Harvard declined to award her a degree because Harvard did not then grant degrees to women. Calkins went on to establish her own laboratory and psychology program at Wellesley College. She became the first woman elected to the American Psychological Association (1905) and to the American Philosophical Association (1918).

In 1902, Harvard grudgingly offered her a degree from Radcliffe College, which she declined as "second-best.

Christine Ladd-Franklin, a student at Vassar College, fulfilled all the requirements for a Ph.D. in mathematics and logic at Johns Hopkins, but again, Hopkins would not grant her the degree because she was a woman. Ladd-Franklin had worked in Germany with George Elias Müller and Hermann von Helmholtz on color perception and presented ten papers at APA meetings between 1894 and1925, but she was denied a full-time academic appointment at Johns Hopkins because her husband was already a professor of mathematics.

Women were not the only "second-class citizens" within the APA. One of the great successes of early American psychologists was persuading boards of trustees about the practical value of psychology. They advocated for psychology to be recognized as an applied science with the potential to alleviate human suffering and social problems, making it of great practical relevance to educators, businessmen, asylum superintendents, and counselors. But a rift grew between academic psychologists and practitioners. Leaders of the APA and heads of the top programs in experimental psychology were reluctant to grant practitioners full status as bona fide scientific psychologists.

In 1904, Lightner Witmer suggested an experimental society that would exclude "half-breeds and extremists." Edward Titchener founded such an elite society, which became known as the Experimentalists. The all-male membership was drawn from the top programs and laboratories. In the face of competition from a rival organization (and because philosophers left in 1902 to form their own association), APA meetings saw declining attendance during the ensuing decades.

Between 1892 and 1930, membership in the APA increased from 42 to 1,101. But this total included 571 non-voting associate members who did not satisfy the rigorous credentials for full membership of the APA—namely, a degree in psychology and publications in professional psychology journals. Despite their social interventionist rhetoric, the officers of the APA were reluctant to grant the status of scientific psychologist to those employed in testing and personnel selection in companies or to those employed as clinical or consulting psychologists in hospitals or private practice.

Concerned about their professional status, consulting psychologists asked the APA to create a certification program to establish their credentials as experts in their field. The APA demurred. Faced with similar concerns, clinical psychologists in 1917 formed the American Association of Clinical Psychologists (AACP). Its goal was to promote professional standards for and legal recognition of clinical psychologists. Robert M. Yerkes, then president of the APA, was deeply concerned about a potential split between the scientific psychologists of the APA and professional practitioners. In 1919, Yerkes persuaded the clinicians to disband the AACP and form the Clinical Section of the APA, where their interests could be better served. In 1921, a consulting section was added, but requests for industrial and educational sections were denied.

The APA did establish a certification program in 1924, but it did little more than award "professional" certificates that had no legal standing. The program was soon abandoned. A year later, the APA introduced an associate membership for those who lacked academic credentials and publications. Because associate membership did not carry voting rights, this change was received less enthusiastically.

Dissatisfied with the lack of progress on professional issues, the New York Association of Consulting Psychologists in 1930 reconstituted itself as the National Association of Consulting Psychologists (ACP). Throughout the decade, the number of applied or consulting psychologists increased faster than the number of academic and scientific psychologists. In 1938, the split that Yerkes had feared finally came to pass. The Clinical Division of the APA and the ACP disbanded and reformed as the American Association of Applied Psychologists (AAAP), with four sections: clinical, consulting, industrial, and educational. The divorce between the academic scientific psychologists and the professional practitioners was complete.

The story might have ended unhappily had it not been for the Second World War, and, once again, Yerkes comes to the rescue. The APA and AAAP joined with the Society for the Psychological Study of Social Issues (SPPSI) and Section I (Psychology) of the American Association for the Advancement of Science to form the Emergency Committee of Psychology, which coordinated psychologists' contributions to the war effort.

Yerkes seized the opportunity. In 1944, he organized a constitutional convention that reorganized the APA. It now encompasses 18 charter divisions, including clinical, consulting, industrial, and educational. (It has since expanded to over 54 divisions.) This reorganization was modeled on the divisional structure of the AACP, which disbanded the same year. The new APA aimed not only to advance "psychology as a science," but also "as a profession and a means of promoting human welfare." The administrative offices of the new APA were housed in the former offices of the OPP in Washington.

Once again, the APA represented both scientists and practitioners, but the tensions remained. The membership of professional psychologists continued to outgrow that of academic and scientific psychologists. This was largely because, after the war, clinical and consulting psychology expanded to meet the psychological demands of returning veterans. Simultaneously, industrial and other applied branches of psychology expanded. Professional psychologists came to dominate the APA presidency and other power structures, formerly the province of academic and scientific psychologists. Dissatisfied with their loss of power and representation, the academics pressed to restructure the APA to better serve their interests. In 1988, when the APA rejected their recommendations, the academic scientific psychologists formed their own society, the American Psychological Society. Now known as the Association for Psychological Science (APS), APS has a membership of around 33,000.

The split between APA and APS was not exhaustive. Many psychologists retained membership in both societies. It also had little impact on APA membership, which grew at a phenomenal rate in the post-war period, from 1,012 in 1945 to 76,000 in 2000. Admittedly, membership peaked in 2008 at 84,000, falling in 2014 to 67,000.

Whether as members of the APA or APS, over the past 125 years, American psychologists have significantly contributed to the advancement of psychological knowledge and the promotion of human welfare, either directly through psychological interventions or indirectly through their lobbying of federal and state agencies.

APA justly celebrates its scientific and professional past and looks forward to "empowering the future of psychology."

American Psychological Association, 2008

NOTE TO GRADUATE STUDENTS AND COLLEAGUES IN PSYCHOLOGY

Dear Graduate Students:

If you are a young professional psychologist or a graduate student in psychology, I would recommend that you review the list of critical historical events and achievements that have occurred over the last two or three centuries because of the studies, research, and writings of psychologists of all persuasions and theoretical orientations.

I would suggest you place a checkmark on all the historical events that you either studied, read about, or personally experienced as a student during your years of training. The length of the list that you check off will give you a sense of the breadth and depth of the field of psychology to which you have been personally exposed and have been part of during your professional training experience.

A count of at least 12 –15 events would be a favorable score relative to your personal exposure to the history and development of the field of psychology. By so doing, psychology as a subject comes into life and has personal, professional, and career impact and meaning for you.

Regards,

Allan G. Hedberg, Ph.D.

PSYCHOLOGY'S MAJOR ACHIEVEMENTS

HISTORICAL CONTRIBUTIONS IN PSYCHOLOGY

1700 - 1800

THE SCIENCE OF PSYCHOLOGY BEGINS HERE

Everything has a beginning. Psychology took its first "Baby steps" in becoming a science.

Ferdinard Ueberwassen

Who said it? Uberwassen (1752–1812) was the first professor of psychological studies, lecturing on the psychological factors operating on a person and influencing their daily experience. He taught at the University of Munster. He is credited with psychology being distinctly recognized as an area of scientific study. Psychology was considered so vital that it was to be taught in all schools and universities as a core independent subject. The year 1783 marked the beginning of psychology being recognized in the academic world.

The next time the field of psychology was considered essential was when scientists were attempting to understand bodily functions in 1854, 70 years later.

The work of Ueberwassen underscores the recognition of the processes of action control and imitation. His studies became the start of behavior, soon being recognized for more than a simple bodily function or response. Psychological factors became a subject of interdisciplinary study. It was like the "kick-off" by Ueberwassen for psychology. His book on empirical psychology was considered the seminal work on the subject at the time.

Additional reading: Schwarz, K., and Pfister, R., Perspective on Psychological Science, Vol. 11., 2016.

WHY ARE WE SO DIFFERENT IN PERSONALITY?

Can a man's skull tell us why we do what we do?

Franz Joseph Gall

Who said it? Dr. Franz Gall, a physician (1758–1828) and a German neuroanatomist and physiologist, pioneered the study of the localization of mental functions and traits. It was he who first led the field in the study of the localization of the brain. He could have just as well been a psychologist. His work essentially mapped the brain into twenty-seven sections, each having a specific function in the conduct of human behavior. More areas were added over time. He mapped the brain in accordance with its contours and any distinguishing features. He became known as the "Skull Reader." He designated the word craniology to define his work and methodology.

Craniology was first called cranioscopy. Gall came upon this idea of relating areas of the brain with certain functions when one of his school chums was known for his skill in memorizing. It was interesting that the same boy had protruding eyes, so Gall came to believe that the area of cortex behind the eyes was the seat of verbal memory. As that area of the brain increased in ability, such as the ability to memorize more, the brain actually expanded in that area in contrast to other areas of the brain. He went on to identify 36 areas of the skull associated with certain characters and mental functions such as benevolence, combativeness, and reference. Parlors sprang up on Broadway, and itinerant craniologists gave skull readings all over the United States. It became the vogue among ordinary folk who sought out this approach to answer life's dilemmas. This is probably not too different from palm reading today.

Gall's pseudo-scientific theory led to the first experimental studies of the localization of brain functions. Although his theory was wrong, it did spring up an area of well-respected scientific and neurological research in the pursuit of brain function related to specific behavioral and personality traits, as well as auditory and visual perception and motor control.

His studies of the brain opened the door to other scientists, such as neurosurgeon Penfield from Montreal, Canada. Penfield proceeded to remove a bit of the brain tissue and then studied how a person would respond.

One area of the brain discovered by this method was the Broca Area, the center of speech, located in the left hemisphere of the brain, slightly forward to the ear. Even to this day, we refer to the Broca area when treating those with language processing problems. Language was considered a high-level brain function. The site of motor control on the left mid-brain and right mid-brain also became an area of such research and identification. Other researchers went on to locate areas of vision, touch, and hearing.

Gall was one of the most valued researchers in psychology and brain function. He was the founder of phrenology. His theory was bizarre, but it did give him and others a starting point for studying the brain more scientifically. His theory has stood the test of time reasonably well. We have studied, because of Gall, the localization of brain functions and have come to understand the cortex as being the seat of intelligence. He significantly moved psychology into a hard science and out of metaphysics and pseudoscience.

The idea that external physical characteristics are linked to psychological traits is not particularly new. Even the Greeks related the size and facial features of a person to their mental abilities and character. Craniology, as it came to be known through the work of Gall, was the doctrine that the contours of the skull are determined by the development of specific areas of the brain and are indicative of character and mental abilities.

Gall was a chronic non-conformist. He was often on the outs with authority. He was vehement in controversy. He was given to blatant womanizing and was considered greedy. For example, he defied convention and charged admission to his scientific demonstrations of brain shapes and functional skills. Many others did likewise.

Overall, he was a first-rate brain anatomist who, by means of his own technique, showed that two halves of the brain are connected to stalks of white matter and that the fibers in the spinal cord cross over when connecting to the lower brain. The larger the amount of gray matter on the cortex or surface of the brain, the more the person is considered to have greater intelligence. He came to this conclusion after examining over 120 skulls.

This research opened the door for much subsequent research, which resulted in the identification of many areas of the brain associated with certain mental functions. This led to the formal and recognized study of craniology. And today, it is known as neuropsychology.

What neuropsychology has become over time is due in part to Gall. His discoveries of the brain structure have stood the test of time. His absurd theory of craniology has led to the experimental study of the localization of the brain and its functions.

His emphasis on the cortex as the seat of intelligence moved psychology farther than ever from metaphysics and closer to empirical science. He deserves a medal and our recognition for his creativity and persistence, despite his personal quirk.

Interestingly, this was the year, 1758, when the smallpox vaccine came out and was made available to the public. Many deaths were recorded after its initial public offering; the famous Jonathan Edwards, the President of Yale, was among them.

Additional Reading: Gall, F., *On the Functions of the Brain and Each of its Parts*, Marsh, Capen, and Lyon, 1835

MENTAL ILLNESS IS TREATABLE

"I determined to try the law of kindness, which. . . has been found to be the most effective control for moral and mental alienation."

Samuel Bayard Woodward

Who said it? Samuel Bayard Woodward (1787–1850) was an American psychiatrist, the first superintendent of the Worcester Lunatic Asylum, and the co-founder and first president of the Association of Medical Superintendents of American Institutions for the Insane (later known as the American Psychiatric Association).

He asserted in one of his reports, "If there is any secret in the management of the insane, it is this: respect them and they will respect themselves; treat them as reasonable beings and they will take every possible pain to show you that they are such; give them your confidence and they will rightly appreciate it and seldom abuse it."

This statement sets the course of the philosophy of treatment through individual psychotherapy based on compassion and optimism, not just medication and/or institutionalization. He also held that the treatment approach should be the same for patients seen in the doctor's office as in the hospital setting.

He objected to the treatment approach of housing the mentally ill in "poor houses" and prisons. Mental illness was viewed as a somatic disease. It was treatable. His approach to treatment was known as "moral therapy," which emphasized the teaching of kindness, compassion, and respect. It was taught through examples and daily interpersonal relationships on the hospital ward with the hospital staff. All staff were to interact with each other in the same manner.

The field of psychology had little input regarding the active treatment of hospitalized patients and their overall care. Any psychological input was limited to the assessment of a patient, not their treatment. Psychologists were allowed to participate in treatment planning but not in the actual treatment process. Psychologists, however, were to be part of and carry out the treatment philosophy based on kindness.

Additional reading: Woodward, S., *Essays on Asylums for the Inebriates*, Forgotten Books, 1835.

HISTORICAL CONTRIBUTIONS IN PSYCHOLOGY

1800 - 1850

THE STIMULUS-RESPONSE CONNECTION

In order for the intensity of a sensation to increase in arithmetical progression,
the stimulus must increase in geometrical progression.

Gustav Fechner

Who said it? Gustav Theodor Fechner (1801–1887) was a German philosopher, physicist, and experimental psychologist. Fechner was born in Poland and came to America to study psychology. He was also an early pioneer in experimental psychology and founded psychophysics. He inspired many 20th-century scientists and psychologists. He was intrigued by the relationship between a stimulus and one's associated personal experience. It was this relationship that contributed to how one reacts to the sensation and the physical intensity of a stimulus. His thinking and research led him to propose what we have come to know as the "Weber-Fechner Law." It demonstrates the non-linear relationship between various psychological events and psychological phenomena.

The Weber-Fechner Law held that the ability to discriminate between two sounds, for example, was known as the "just noticeable difference." It promoted a huge amount of research over the years, which formed the focus of early psychology in 1854 and thereafter. For example, he studied motivational, physical, and social factors and their interaction with each other when judging an event to determine the just-noticeable difference operating between any two stimuli.

Fechner helped us understand how we deal with life events. It is not just the event, but the personal experiences we bring to the event. Hence, we draw upon our past experiences when we act upon some stimulus event, such as flashing lights or intermittent sounds. The greater the intensity of the stimulus event, the more it draws us into an action mode. Essentially, our background and prior experiences play a large role in determining how we react to a stimulus event.

Fechner was recognized as one of the three fathers of psychology, along with Webner and Wundt.

Additional Reading: Fechner, G.T., *The Little Book of Life After Death,* Black Letter Press, 1836

PURSUE EDUCATION

Be a pioneer; pursue your area of study with passion.

Christine Ladd-Franklin

Who said it? Dr. Ladd-Franklin (1847–1930) was a psychologist, logician, and mathematician. She was properly called Kitty. She was a precocious child. Her father encouraged her to pursue education. She enrolled in classes designed to prepare her for an education at Harvard. For a brief time, she was a schoolteacher. Her mother was active in the movement for women's rights. She followed in her mother's footsteps and attended many school events with her mother.

Although she earned her Ph.D. degree from Johns Hopkins University, the school refused to honor her for the fact that she was a woman. However, the school did honor her for her work and degree 40 years later, at age 78.

Women were prohibited from working in physics laboratories in the 19th century, so she chose mathematics. However, she preferred to study physics. She wrote and often spoke of the oppression women experienced and the need for increased levels of independence and recognition, especially in an educational setting.

Her psychological research was on vision, and she developed a theory of color vision. It was based on evolution. She stated that some animals are colorblind and assumed that achromatic vision appeared first in evolution and color came later. She stated that color vision occurs in three stages: achromatic vision, blue-yellow sensitivity, and green-red sensitivity. They developed sequentially through evolution. Black/white colorblindness is rare because it develops first in the evolutionary process.

She was included in Who's Who in America. She was a prominent member of the Women's Rights Movement. She joined the American Psychological Association in 1893.

Additional reading: Ladd-Franklin, C., *Color and Color Theories*, Harcourt, Brace and Co., 1929.

WHAT IS A PERSONAL EXPERIENCE?

We speak of virtue, honor, and reason,
but our thoughts do not translate
any one of these concepts into substance.

Whilhelm Wundt

Who said it? Wundt (1832–1920) was not only an early German psychologist but also the founder of the first psychology laboratory devoted to the systematic study of psychological ideas and phenomena. He was the first person to call himself a "psychologist." In his laboratory, various psychological phenomena were elevated within the overall field of a growing physical science. He was recognized as one of the three fathers of psychology.

Under Wundt, psychology came to recognize that a person contributes his own personal experience to his response to any given event or observation. One's firsthand experiences come to be real and influential, but they are not substance. Rather, personal experiences come to be recognized as constructs or phenomena, just as worthy of specific study as any other area of study.

Many of his students became psychologists because of his teaching and laboratory research. Indeed, he was a role model for early psychology.

Additional reading: Wundt, W., *Outlines of Psychology*, Nabu Press, 1896.

THE LEARNING EXPERIENCE

Everyone should do at least two things each day that he hates to do —just for practice.

William James

Who said it? William James (1842–1910) was not only a psychologist in the 1800's but a philosopher as well. After he graduated with a degree in psychological studies, he taught at Harvard. He was the first psychology educator to offer a formal psychology course in the United States. He is often referred to as the "Father of American Psychology." He is known for such ideas as streams of consciousness, the theory of the self, brain usage, the pragmatic theory of truth, and determinism. He is among the 100 most well-known psychologists of the 19th century.

James was a very studious individual and devoted long hours to the study of psychology, philosophy, and a variety of other subjects such as biology and religion. This is not an uncommon pattern of interest for scholars. He believed strongly that you learn from what you do. If you keep repeating the same thing all the time, you will not learn anything new. However, he encouraged people to engage in the practice of doing something that they did not do very often or that they did not like to even do. By doing so, learning will occur. He stated that sometimes the greatest learning experience comes from adverse events and challenges.

He also believed that learning isn't just about concepts and subjects. What is most important is learning about yourself, your own strengths and weaknesses, and how to live a functional life. His challenge was to do something new each day. To get out of the rut you're in. Only then will you become a fully developed individual. Life then becomes enjoyable. It requires getting out of your comfort zone, expanding your life, and changing your daily experiences.

James defined the subject of psychology as the feeling, acts, and experiences of individuals in relation to what they consider to be divine. His broad topics included the religion of the healthy mind, the sixth soul, the divided self and its unification, conversion, saintliness, and mysticism. He drew much from an entire range of world literature.

He published his famous 1200-page text, *The Principles of Psychology*. It became a classic. He influenced many students over his 35 years of teaching as well as his writings. His influence continues today.

While James lived and taught over a hundred years ago, the lives of his students at that time who adopted his approach to life and daily behavior succeeded, expanded their life experiences, and achieved remarkable things. Likewise, today we excel, we achieve, and we enjoy life more fully as we reach beyond our comfort zone and beyond our daily and traditional experiences and behavior patterns.

He also worked on problems in the workplace. Employee testing and exams were his interests.

Additional reading: James, W., *The Variety of Religious Experiences, E: A Study in Human Nature*, Harvard University Press, 1985.

HOW TO DEVELOP POSITIVE BEHAVIOR

Use praise to encourage and support desired behaviors.

Edward Thorndike

Who said it? Lea Edward Thorndike (1847–1949) was born in Willamsburg, Massseucettes, and was educated at Wesleyan University and Columbia Teachers College. He taught his full career at Columbia.

His experimental work was on animals and focused on the learning process. He coined the Law of Effect as the basic learning process. Learning is the process of connecting a stimulus with a response. A pleasant effect results in learning occurring. He also formulated the Law of readiness and the Law of Exercise.

Essentially, learning requires a readiness for learning, and it requires the exercise of repeated practice of a newly learned skill or concept. It was a way of thinking about learning as a result of consequences. His subjects were mostly cats.

He was well known for his Word Books used in education by teachers, including what words to use and when.

Additional reading: Thorndike, E., *Educational Psychology: A Briefer Course*, Routledge, 1913.

WHAT IS ADOLESCENCE?

Adolescence is when the very worst
and best impulses in the human soul
struggle against each other for possession.

G. Stanley Hall

Who said it? Dr. Hall (1844–1924) was interested in human development throughout his life. He founded the first psychological laboratory in America for the study of psychology. He was the first president of the American Psychological Association. He served throughout the 19th century. He had deep roots in Americanism. Interestingly, his grandmother came to America on the Mayflower.

He was a convinced hereditarian. He taught the subject and encouraged one's heredity to be considered in psychological studies of human behavior. Also, he held that the war pushed psychology into the field of applied science rather than pure science.

To be sure, Hall underscored that adolescence is a very tough time in life. It's a time of significant struggles, advancements, and setbacks. Adolescence is a time of learning: learning to accept success and failure, learning how to achieve success, and coping with defeat. From this line of thinking and research, he advocated for studies on the thinking patterns of schoolchildren. This line of studies soon led to the establishment of the field of child psychology.

Additional reading: Hall, G.S., *Confessions of a Psychologist*, Nabu Press, 2010.

HOW WE LEARN

Facts are the errors of science. Without them, a man of science can never rise.

Ivan Pavlov

Who said it? Dr. Pavlov (1849–1936) was not a psychologist but impacted the field of psychology more than most psychologists. His impact relates to how we learn. He might as well have been a psychologist. He would have been a good one. While his father wanted him to be a priest, Ivan abandoned the seminary training opportunity and transferred to the University of St. Petersburg to study natural sciences, and then later to the Academy of Medical Surgery, where he gained his doctorate.

His educational and career-formation story was strikingly similar to that of Martin Luther. He soon came to teach as a professor at the Military Medical Center while conducting his research on dogs. That is where he conducted his famous research into the digestive secretion of dogs. The learning principle of conditioned learning, for which he is famous, was surreptitiously discovered while conducting his research on dog salivation. He became famous for this research on dogs (Pavlov's Dogs) and how they learned by associating two events occurring simultaneously.

He began to study the links between various stimuli and the responses that they elicited. He demonstrated that a learned response could be mental as well as physical by conducting experiments in which various kinds of stimuli were assimilated. The principle became known as "classical or Pavlovian conditioning." It was groundbreaking. It was these steps that allowed psychology to emerge as a truly scientific rather than a philosophical discipline. The work of Pavlov had a hugely influential impact on other psychologists, such as John Watson and B.F. Skinner. Pavlov was certainly known as one of the "building blocks" of modern psychology.

Pavlov's research led to our understanding of "associative learning," which is now known as classical conditioning. This is a basic form of learning. We learn by associating two or more things together by their common identity or use, such as salt and pepper.

For Pavlov, it was the association of a ringing bell and the dog salivating. Soon the dog came to salivate when a bell was rung at a particular or highly similar frequency. This research started a whole new approach to learning and helped shape the style of teaching and learning of the day.

If you are in the process of learning new information, use the classical conditioning approach. Link or pair things that go together. See the association between things, experiences, and ideas. By so doing, you will become a better learner and achiever. This is one major way to learn how to learn.

Finally, Pavlo's work placed him in an integral role in making psychology more of a scientific and rigorous discipline.

Additional reading: Pavlo, I., *Conditioned Refluxes in Psychiatry*, 1941.

HISTORICAL CONTRIBUTIONS IN PSYCHOLOGY

1850 -1900

LEARNING AND MEMORY GO TOGETHER

Memory is the treasure house of the mind, wherein
the monuments there are kept and preserved.

Hermann Ebbinghaus

Who said it? Hermann Ebbinghaus (1850–1909) was German by birth. He studied philosophy at the age of 17. After his studies, he moved to Berlin, then to France, and finally to England. While in Berlin, he established two psychology laboratories at the university and founded an academic journal. He continued to teach at the university until his premature death at age 59. He became the first psychologist to systematically and empirically study learning and memory. Before that, memory was studied and understood by philosophers.

It was Ebbinghaus who helped us understand the memory process. He developed the "forgetting graph," which charted the speed of forgetting. It was this graph that spurred much research on memory functions such as the acquisition of information, short-term memory, long-term memory, memory recall, and memory recognition. His research also contributed much to our understanding of the brain and how it facilitates learning, memory, and recall. He demonstrated that repeated learning sessions over a longer interval of time improve memory retention on any subject, for example.

His studies of memory were mathematically recorded to see if memory followed verifiable patterns. He served as his own subject initially. He found that he could remember meaningful material, such as a poem, ten times more easily than any nonsense list. Also, the more times something was repeated, the less time was needed to reproduce the memorized material. Further, the first few repetitions proved the most effective in memorizing a list.

He found that there was a very typical and rapid loss of recall in the first hour, followed by a slightly slower loss thereafter. Nine hours was the time limit when most forgetting was demonstrated. After twenty-four hours, about two-thirds of anything memorized is forgotten. He plotted his experiences on a graph known as "The Forgetting Curve."

The Forgetting Curve begins with a sharp drop and then has a shallow slope. Items towards the beginning and the end of a series of items to be memorized were most easily remembered. His forgetting curve underscored what became known as the "Serial-Position Effect" of learning.

His work helped establish psychology as a scientific discipline. His meticulous methods were followed by others engaged in psychological experimentation, even to this very day.

Additional reading: Ebbinghaus, H., *Psychology: An Elementary Textbook,* Forgotten Books, 1932.

MY STRENGTH COMES

Out of your vulnerabilities comes your strength.

Sigmund Freud

Who said it? Dr. Sigmund Freud (1856–1939) is well known for his independent views on the mind and how it functions. He viewed the mind as having three components: the Id, the Ego, and the Superego. Each part had its own function but worked in coordination to bring about a well-functioning human being. However, whenever there was dissonance among the three parts, the person experienced some form of anxiety, stress, or mental illness. Long periods of treatment were considered the only way to right the wrongs in the life of a patient.

The therapist believed that the patient's parents, particularly the mother, had mistreated him or her to a large extent. Mothers are often viewed as harsh, meanspirited, and inconsistent. Hence, patients often reflect this parental influence in their mental illnesses.

Introspection was a key process by which patients came to understand themselves and others. It became a major tool in psychotherapy for patients in their pursuit of self-understanding.

Similarly, hypnosis was used to assist patients with pain relief rather than using anesthesia. Hypnosis also became used as a technique to help patients explore their inner selves, especially when they became stuck in their personal pursuit of their inner selves. Why it worked for Freud is still largely a mystery. He put much faith in it as a technique.

Dreams became a fascination for Freud. He used it extensively in therapy. It was his way of getting the patient to explore his inner self and uncover deep emotional trauma. He became quite skilled in the art of dream interpretation. He wrote a major treatise on the topic.

Freud was also interested in the distinction between mental illness, common distress, and emotional disturbance. He lectured on the topic when he once visited America.

He wrote extensively. It's fascinating to read his personal account of how Hitler extradited him from Germany.

Freud was identified as one of psychology's most famous psychologists, but also the most notorious. His ideas were and continue to be controversial. He was considered the most influential thinker in psychology. Many became associated with him and later broke away from his ideas. For example, Adler broke away and later developed what is now called "individual psychology." Adler influenced many significant psychologists thereafter, as did most of the students and followers of Freud who broke with him personally and from his theories of personality and human behavior. He is well-known for his death instinct.

And he was also known for his view on the death instinct.

He was known to have much conflict with the political system of his day. Hitler was afraid of Freud and his teachings. Freud gave Hitler much to fear. Hitler eventually won by pressuring Freud to leave Germany and putting a high price tag on his departure from Germany.

Additional reading: Freud, S., *The Interpretation of Dreams*, General Press, 1899.

SOCIAL CHANGE

Whenever a great movement sweep through a civilized world, it generally starts with the recognition of a great social wrong and the enthusiasm for a change.

Hugo Munsterburg

Who said it? Munsterburg (1863–1916) was the first to demonstrate that psychology had a role to play in law, business, and a variety of other areas of study. He was born on June 1, 1863, in Danzig, Prussia, which is modern-day Gdansk, Poland. His father, Moritz Munsterberg, had two sons from a previous marriage. Hugo's mother, Minna Anna Bernhardhi, was a cousin of Moritz's first wife. Anna Bernhardhi gave birth to Hugo and Oscar. All four boys were raised together in the same household as brothers.

Moritz was in the lumber business. Anna was a musician and artist who continued to work while raising the four children. She had an appreciation for art, literature, and ethics. After Anna's untimely death, 12-year-old Hugo focused on self-discipline and education under the guidance of his father. He graduated from the Academic Gymnasium Danzig in 1882, two years after the premature death of his father.

Munsterberg went on to study medicine after staying on for only one semester at his university for the study of French literature. His interest in psychology was rejuvenated when he heard Wilhelm Wundt speak. He went on to earn his Ph.D. in psychology in 1885 from the University of Leipzig and his medical degree in 1887 from the University of Heidelberg. He taught many prominent psychologists, including Mary Calkins. He spent most of his career in Europe.

Munsterberg taught at the University of Freiburg until he was offered a position to be chairman of the psychology lab at Harvard. He only spoke and wrote in German upon his arrival but quickly picked up English. He was quickly offered a permanent position due to his popularity with the students and his enticing lectures.

He disagreed with Sigmund Freud's theories of the unconscious. He did not accept the notion of an unconscious. This created much intellectual curiosity on the part of his students of psychology.

Munsterberg's initial work related to sensations. Later on, he moved to study applied psychology. It was Munsterburg who opened the field of psychological thought and study to the real world of social and business discourse. Psychology, as a result, came to play a significant role in human affairs. It marks the beginning of psychology being recognized as an applied science itself.

The empirical evidence he construed from his studies was applied to other branches of psychology as well. For example, his work in forensic psychology led to the discovery of how people witness a distinct event and testify. Eyewitness forensic testimony is a major area of study today, thanks to Hugo. So is the industry of filming and criminology.

Munsterberg is most known for his work in applied psychology, particularly in industry and clinical psychology. In simple terms, industrial psychology is the study of how people work together and apply psychology concepts to work-related situations. Munsterberg is considered the father of industrial psychology because he was the first to apply psychology to the work industry. Munsterberg's work uncovered hiring techniques in the work environment. He produced a system that prioritized hiring the best candidate for a job to increase productivity and reduce exhaustion among other workers. In addition, he suggested using the staff member's strengths as an advantage, placing workers in the most efficient positions. His idea about hiring was to first hire a qualified person and then assign them a duty to perform based on their skills.

Hugo Munsterberg is considered the father of industrial psychology for his work and research in the psychology of individuals placed in a work environment. He developed tactics that increased productivity and decreased fatigue. His work in industrial psychology opened the door for corporations to hire the best possible candidate by playing to the advantage of the individual. Productivity increased by hiring 'the best man for the job.'

However, during World War I, he received backlash for supporting Germany, his home country. He died unexpectedly during a lecture on December 16, 1916.

Additional reading: Munsterberg, H., *Psychology and Industrial Efficiency*, 1913.

A VIVID IMAGINATION IS HELPFUL

I have a vivid sense of the concreteness of psychology and of the immediate reality of finite individual minds.

Mary Whinton Calkins

Who said it? Dr. Calkins (1863–1930) was an American philosopher and psychologist. She completed her Ph.D. degree at Harvard but did not have the full support of the faculty because she was a woman. She did not accept the award she had earned. She was refused a Ph.D. by Harvard University because of her gender. The president at Harvard opposed the idea that women could learn in the same room as men. She studied at Harvard as a guest, not as a registered student. Many famous psychologists, including James and Musterberg, refused to grant her a degree because she was a woman.

She also attended Smith College. As a student, she worked under Hugo Munsterberg and William James. She taught at Wellesley College. She established the first psychological laboratory for women at Wellesley. Her classes were very popular among students. She has published four books and one hundred papers. She always worked and strived for equality, even though she was not granted equality while at Harvard.

She studied memory and the concept of the self. She worked on information theory and conducted research on memory, dreams, and the self. She is known for the formulation of paired associate learning.

One of her research studies was recording, throughout a period of time, her dreams. She recorded 205 dreams. Upon awakening, she would immediately write down her dreams as she remembered them. She then rated them as slight, trivial, or significant. She then recorded the dream by type and discovered elements of various emotions. She concluded that dreams merely reproduced, in general, the persons and places of recent sense perception and that dreams are associated with those that are of paramount significance in one's waking experience. Freud drew upon her research on dreams when he authored his book on the topic.

To fulfill her professional goals and pursuits, she went to Germany and studied with Hugo Munsterberg, who opened the laboratory doors to her without hesitation. Women were recognized in the profession in Germany. She was welcomed in his laboratory and thrived there as a professional woman.

She is quoted as having said, "Beyond all else, I have a vivid sense of the concreteness of psychology and of the immediate reality of finite individual minds with their thoughts and feelings. In this statement, she blends philosophy and psychology, her two areas of study, research, and teaching. Psychology is considered to be the study and science of the self.

She served as president of the American Psychological Association and the American Philosophical Association.

She invented the paired-associate technique and contributed much to our understanding of dreams. She advocated for self-psychology and wrote more than 100 professional papers on psychology and philosophy.

Additional reading: Calkins, Mary, *The Good Man and the Good: An Introduction to Ethics*, Kessinger Legacy Reprints, 1918.

MY WORLD IS UP TO ME

The world is as large as the range of one's interests.
A narrow-minded person has a narrow outlook.

Joseph Jastrow

Who said it? Joseph Jastrow (1863–1944) was the first student of psychology to earn a Ph.D. in psychology. He was Polis born. He graduated from Clark University in 1893. He was a student of war and the Nazi mind. He later taught at the University of Wisconsin. He worked to popularize psychology through his writings, teaching, public lectures, and the writing of newspaper columns for over 50 years in the early 1900s. He wrote on popular topics of the day and tried to interest his readers in the psychology of human behavior.

He held to the view that our world is in our hands and the future is ours if we have an open mind and an inquisitive mind. The world is larger and greater, and we can know it. However, we set our own limits on the world we live in and experience. Actually, the world is an open place for our exploration and intrigue. What keeps us withholding is our fear of the unknown and the unexperienced. When we push back on our fear, we can explore and experience life beyond our self-defined boundaries. We may need a mentor or coach if we want to go beyond our current self-imposed limits. We all prefer to live within our comfort zone of daily life. It is when we breakout and explore the world beyond that we really come to live life fully.

He believed that risk-taking was necessary. Curiosity and an inquisitive mind are necessary to experience life beyond. Getting out of one's shell is a special skill. It takes boldness and assertive living skills.

He also worked on the phenomenon of optical illusions. They have become well-known as Jastrow Illusions. He believed that everyone had their own, often incorrect, harsh conceptions about psychology. One of his ultimate goals was to use a scientific method to identify truth from error and educate the layperson through speaking tours, print media, and the radio.

As part of his optical illusion, he had a great deal of interest in perception, especially eyesight. He thought that eyesight was more complex than the camera and that the mental processing of images was central to the interpretation of the world. He believed that what people saw also depended on their emotional state and their surroundings. He found that the autograph would detect unconscious movement of the hand, and the magnitude of the effect varied across individuals, especially in children. Their movements were much more random than adults'.

He was also interested in the dreams of the blind. He found that after six years of age, people still had dreams, but if they lost their eyesight before five, they could not. He concluded that sight was not innate and that significant mental development occurred between ages five and seven. He noted that hearing, not sensation, was the primary sense of the blind in both waking and dreaming. He collected many first-hand accounts of dreams from visually impaired people, including Helen Keller.

He was critical of psychoanalysis as unscientific and pseudo-science. Along this line, he published the book *The House That Freud Built.*

Additional reading: Jastrow, J., *Fact and Fable in Psychology,* Houghton Mifflin, 1900.

CALM COMES FROM THE FAMILIAR

People experience the "glow of warmth" when they are in the presence of familiar things.

Edward Bradford Titchener

Who said it? Titchener (1867–1927), born in England, studied experimental psychology under Wundt. He was one of Wundt's most advanced and accomplished students.

He undertook a remarkable career in the teaching of psychology. He presented himself as "the professor" to his students. He was a very formal man and taught psychology in a very structured manner while wearing his doctoral robes.

He subsequently moved to the United States in 1892 and became known as the founder of structural psychology. He was widely known and admired as a professor. He wrote numerous textbooks on psychology.

Focused on breaking down human consciousness into the smallest possible elements. He coined the word "empathy."

Titchener viewed the experiences of man in elementary structures. It was based on introspection. Structural psychology conflicted with behaviorism, which at the time was growing in popularity. In his research, he would describe familiar firsthand experiences as a "warm glow" experience.

Additional reading: Titchener, E., *Lectures on the Elementary Psychology of Feelings and Attention*, The Macmillan Company, 1908.

PSYCHOLOGY GAINS RECOGNITION

Clinical psychology is a fully professional helping science.

Lightner Whitmer

Who said it? Whitmer (1867–1956) focused his professional life and research efforts on the application of psychology to human problems. He was one of the early psychologists who refocused the profession on applied issues of life rather than abstract ideas and concepts of basic science. He opened his research laboratory in 1896. In this way, he followed the lead of Munsterberg and his application of psychology to business and commerce. Also, Whitmer was the psychologist who applied the principles of psychology to school-related problems in learning and behavior.

He held the position that applied science and pure science were the same, or at least interrelated. One fosters the other. He thought that the contribution psychology makes to the advancement of humanity will determine how far it advances. He also held that psychology had a major influence upon advancements in education, speech correction, social adjustment, industrial problems, and vocational choice, to name a few. Hence, psychology was a major field of study in and of itself, but it was also important for a multitude of other fields of study to advance.

Additional reading: Whitmer, L., *The Psychology Clinic*, Vol. 1-3, 1906.

What is really important?

Be remembered for the lives saved and your influence on others.

Karl Bonhoeffer

Who said it? Karl Bonhoeffer (1868–1949) was a Professor of Psychiatry at Breslau University. While anti-Semitism was functioning well during his day, he regarded it as an unsuitable criterion for personal politics. In contrast, he hired a considerable number of Jewish assistants as staff, about thirty altogether. Unfortunately, many of his staff were persecuted in 1933, when massive persecution by the Germans set in. They were persecuted for their political views. Some were able to immigrate. Most were racially persecuted. He worked diligently to extend contracts for his students against the odds of the German system at the time of Semitism. He even went as far as to falsify medical documents to gain the students favor with the German army. As time went on, most of them had to immigrate to stay alive. They went to other countries and advanced there because of his recommendations. His commitment to his students and the staff members resulted in some of them escaping death, which otherwise would have been their fault.

He lectured frequently, connecting psychiatry, psychology, and neurology. An award was named after him, the Karl Bonhoeffer Prize, which takes place every three years. The prize was to read a paper dealing with the subject connecting psychiatry and neurology. He strongly opposed the thinking and writings of Freud and many of the other analytic thinkers of the day. Empirical scientific explanation of human behavior was his thinking and approach to understanding human behavior. He died as a result of a stroke.

Bonhoeffer and his wife came from an extensive lineage of royalty. Perhaps Dr. Bonhoeffer is best known for his son, Dietric. Dietrich was an intellectual, writer, and artist who became involved in a complicated plot to assassinate Hitler. Unfortunately, the plot failed. Dietrich was imprisoned and lived in a concentration camp for many years, eventually being assassinated by hanging. The irony is that he was hanged one month prior to the war ending and Hitler surrendering to the Allied Forces. Although he was dead, Dietrich authored many books and treatises that have outlived him and have been read by millions of people around the world, as is still the case today. He has had a profound influence on political, social, religious, and artistic thought.

Additional reading: Metaxas, E., *Bonhoeffer: Pastor, Prophet, Spy,* Thomas Nelsen, 2010.

THE DEPTH OF THE HUMAN MIND

Nothing in the world is as compelling to the emotions as the mind of another human being.

Margaret Floy Washburn

Who said it? Dr. Washburn (1871–1939) was the first female American psychologist who devoted her life to the teaching of psychology in the late 1800s and early 1900s. In those days, a female professor could not be married, so she remained single and went on to distinguish herself as one of America's great professors of psychology.

According to Dr. Washburn, her way of thinking about another individual was one of compelling intrigue and served as the basis of her psychological studies. It became her professional obsession.

We are still intrigued by the mind, thinking patterns, and potential of each other in the same way that Dr. Washburn focused her psychological interest and research. Her studies of the human mind, with its potential and capabilities, became her obsession. Interestingly, she even became interested in why people are obsessive-compulsive.

Obsessions can be good or bad. It is important to know the difference and when an obsession is dysfunctional. Good obsessions are often associated with achievement, accomplishments, and progress. We all need to be a little obsessive. Keep it controlled. Keep it constructive. Keep it reasonable.

She also studied animal behavior and motor development. Accordingly, she never ran out of research issues to pursue. She stood as an equal among the male psychologists of her day.

She served as President of the American Psychological Association during her active career in 1921.

Additional reading: Furumoto and Scarborough, *Women in Psychology*, American Psychologist, 1986, pp. 35-42.

PERSONALITY IS BASED ON CONFLICT

The reason some people do not see God is because they will not look low enough.

Carl Jung

Who said it? Carl Jung (1875–1961) is famous for his theory on the various levels and complications of a person's life. They are part of an overall picture, like a puzzle, that needs to be understood and put together properly. An individual's history and firsthand experiences are critical to a full life and quality of life as an adult. His primary practice and contributions came in the first half of the 1900s.

Jung also held religious and mystical convictions and a belief in the collective unconscious. This was a state of mind common to all individuals. After having been an enthusiastic follower of Freud for years, his thinking on the topic became a point of contention with Freud.

To be sure, Jung understood that life is complex and that we cannot understand something positive without having experienced something negative. Happiness is only experienced, understood, and appreciated when one experiences an unpleasant perspective of a life of unhappiness, sadness, regret, trauma, grief, and unfulfillment.

Jung's theory is based on the concept that to understand light, we also have to experience darkness. Both are part of the human experience. Both are real. Both shape the individual from childhood. A person cannot avoid darkness, error, sadness, or despair. One can only appreciate the absence of such emotional states when life is lived fully and exponentially.

As it has been true throughout history, it will be true throughout the millennium to come. Darkness begets life. Sadness begets happiness. Life is a complex of opposites. We need to appreciate both ends of the spectrum as vital to the daily living experience for all of us. Further, the mind, in its fullness, oscillates between sense and nonsense, between right and wrong, and between light and darkness.

Accordingly, we are to embrace both extremes. We are not to condemn darkness, hurt, sadness, or trauma, as such experiences bring us to a closer understanding of the opposite, light, truth, understanding, contentment, and happiness.

Jung and Freud were friends initially and often shared experiences and ideas. However, Carl Jung eventually came to disagree with Freud's central doctrine of the sexual origin of neurosis. Their thinking on the matter eventually became a source of contention between them. Jung gradually drew away from Freud, and in 1914, he formally broke with the Freudian movement and founded his own. This was similar to other therapists at the time, such as Otto Rank, who also drew away from Freud.

Jung soon developed his own theories of human behavior. This also strained the relationship between the two men, and their relationship finally ended in 1926. It was recognized that he did have trouble holding his followers as long-term friends. You either agreed with him or you didn't. The quality of the friendship followed suit.

Jung portrayed personality as shaped largely by the interplay of the opposing inherent tendencies towards assertiveness and passivity, introversion and extroversion, and a conflict between experience and the collective unconscious. He wrote extensively about these ideas.

Henry Murray, a psychologist, is the subject of the tale. He believed that he had been subject to torture from a demon. He traveled to Zurich, Switzerland, to connect with Carl Jung and spent three weeks in daily sessions and long weekends of psychotherapy. He states that he emerged as a newborn man. He recalls the experience as "an explosive experience" for him.

He was also one of the early therapists who interpreted elements of fairy tales as manifestations of universal fears and desires. He viewed psychotherapy as an "explosive experience" based on his own personal experience. Psychotherapy was, accordingly, growing in acceptance.

His most controversial idea was that of the collective unconscious. It was considered a mysterious force that controlled our actions. It suggests that all humans share a common psychic realm where instincts and memories are stored. It is transmitted through brain structures and is the deepest layer of the psychic. This mysterious psychological phenomenon expresses itself through certain archetypes. These were patterns of behavior that turn on and respond to certain situations that arise. It was considered the source of all myths and legends. It was like a giant pool of knowledge we all have access to. He went on to say that we are all connected to this pool and can draw from it whenever necessary. Some people are more attuned to the collective unconscious than others. They were considered psychically gifted and creative geniuses. Such people can tap into the collective unconscious and draw upon its power to achieve great things. The collective unconscious is part of the mind that all humans share. He was Freud's most famous and controversial student. He was always interested in the study of mythology and religion. Many have written books about him on topics such as memories, dreams, and reflections.

Additional reading: Jung, K., *Karl Jung in His Own Words*, Goodread Books, 2011.

CONSIDER FREEDOM

The truth will set you free. And truth has a name.

Robert Yerkes

Who said it? Robert Yerkes (1876–1956) was an American ethologist, eugenicist, and primatologist, as well as a psychologist. The behavior of animals was an area of fascination for him.

He developed a test of intelligence, the Alpha and Beta test, used in WWI to measure intelligence. The military was forbidden to hire someone whose intelligence measured less than an 83 on a scale of 100. He believed it measured native intelligence, unaffected by culture. It became known as a "culture-free" test. The whole field of intelligence measurement has advanced because of him. It was a pivotal moment in the history of psychology.

He is best known for his behavioral research with anthropoid apes, chimpanzees, and gorillas. All of his papers, documents, and writings—even notes—were kept and stored in filing drawers and boxes. After his death, his wife donated them to the Yale Sterling Library in meticulous categorical order by subject and topic. He was a note-taker and record-keeper, to be sure.

Comparative psychology was his other area of research interest. Topics studied were instincts in animals, social behavior of animals, learning styles, and adaptation of animals, to name a few.

Of particular interest was his formation of the Yerkes-Dodson Law. It held that performance increases with physiological or mental arousal up to a point. But when arousal is too high, performance decreases. The bell-shaped curve is the image he used to present the idea to the scientific community.

Additional reading: Yerkes, R., *The Dancing Mouse: A Guide to the Study of Animal Behavior*, Kessinger Publishing, 1907.

MEASURE IT

There is nothing about an individual as important as his IQ, except possibly his morals.

Lewis Terman

Who said it? Lewis Terman (1877–1956), was the founder of the famous Terman-Binet IQ test. The children used to develop the test by signing a contract that bonded them for the rest of their lives, so repeated testing over time could take place. These kids were popularly known as the "Terman's Termites."

Test development is an art. It has definite guidelines that must be followed carefully and uniformly. It was then, through systematic age-based test administration, that subsequent individuals were measured on a particular dimension. Testing of all sorts became a domain of psychology, especially performance tasks. The test became heavily used in education, military selection, and business-related choices and decisions.

Children are taught how to take tests and not let them create a high degree of anxiety. Test scores are indicators, guides, and pointers, but not absolutes. They give an indication of what one can do and pursue and those areas to avoid. His basic belief was that intelligence is inherited. His early studies focused on gifted children.

Terman was also deeply involved in the eugenics movement. It was a set of beliefs and practices that aimed to improve the genetic quality of the human population, playing a significant role in the history and cultural development of the states from the 19th century to the mid-20th century. Intellectuals of the progressive era promoted the cause more and more. The role was to extensively improve genetic quality. It has been argued that genetic eugenics is more about preserving the position of the dominant group and the population. Scholarly research determined that people who found themselves targeting eugenics movements were those who were seen as unfit for society: the poor, the disabled, the mentally ill, and various specific communities of color. Many fell victim to the eugenic sterilization initiatives. Now it is associated with racism, and as a movement, it has become extinct.

Besides Terman, the movement was led by Sir Francis Galton in the mid-1880s. Galton studied the upper classes of Britain and arrived at the conclusion that their social position could be attributed to a superior genetic make-up. American eugenicists tended to believe in the genetic superiority of the Nordic Germanic and Anglo-Saxon people, and they supported the forceful sterilization of the poor, disabled, and immoral.

Funding for the eugenics movement came from the Carnegie Institution, the Rockefeller Foundation, and the Harimn Railroad Fortune. J.H. Kellogg also contributed. One of the most prominent feminists to champion the eugenics agenda was Margaret Sanger, the leader of the American birth control movement and the founder of Planned Parenthood.

Additional reading: Terman, L., *The Uses of Intelligence Tests*, Houghton Mifflin, 1916.

THINK

Our thoughts contribute to our behavior and soon become behavioral patterns.

John B. Watson

Who said it? Watson (1878–1958) was the father of behaviorism and an American psychologist. He left psychology and entered the field of business advertising. One of his contracts was with a cigarette company, and his charge was to get more women to smoke. He accomplished his assignment by applying the rule of successive approximation, drawing upon his earlier psychological research in the field of perception.

His idea was to print posters with an image of a package of cigarettes and a man smoking in the forefront and an image of a woman in the background looking at the pack of cigarettes and the man smoking. Over time, the poster was gradually changed, with the woman placed in a more forward position in the picture and holding a cigarette. Eventually, the image was changed, so the woman in the picture was actually smoking. This process is known as "progressive approximation."

His applied use of the mental process of thought led him to the concept of advocating for thinking before acting. It was IBM that picked up on the idea of thinking and made it their company's motto. Others then adopted the motto for various purposes. The motto emphasized the idea being studied by earlier psychologists in considering how one's personal experience, even his thoughts, eventually contributed to one's behavior.

Based on Watson's research, we are all subject to social influence, especially subtle influence. We need to be aware of this subtle influence and better manage how we relate to others, especially if they are different from us.

His writings established the school of behavioral psychology.

Additional reading: Watson, J. *Behaviorism*, 1924.

WHERE ARE WE GOING?

How one behaves is more important than how we come to understand or explain the behavior.

Clark L. Hull

Who said it? Clark Hull (1884–1952) was a leader among leaders. He was the man for psychology at a time when leadership and a vision were definitely needed. Essentially, he put psychology on the "scientific map" and mapped out its future direction. This has been true throughout the ages. The call for a man to stand in the gap is time-honored; Clark was the man for psychology. We marched forward under his leadership.

Clark was a man of achievement as well as a leader. He designed the drive-reduction approach to learning. The theory held that no learning occurs unless a drive produces tension, and the tension impels the organism into some type of activity or action to procure a reward that would reduce the drive and satisfy the related need. It was the reduction of the drive that acted as reinforcement for that behavior. And it was the reinforcement that assured that the behavior would occur again in the future if that or a similar situation once again occurred. It was a stimulus-response relationship followed by a reinforcer. In that context, future behavior became predictable, and current behavior patterns became understandable.

In formulating his psychological theories, he related them to mathematical formulas and expressions. He was also one of the first to scientifically study hypnosis. He was a prolific writer and wrote 10 books over his career.

Additional reading: Hull, C., *Hypnosis and Suggestibility*, Crown House Publishing, 1933.

YOU HAVE THE PSYCHOLOGICAL POINT OF VIEW

The statement was made by Titchener of Boring when he was considering a change in studies from engineering to psychology based on his enrollment in an introductory psychology class taught by Titchener. Many psychologists over the years had that "point of view" and thrived.

Edward Boring

Edward Boring (1886–1968) was a renowned educator and scientist. Cornell was his alma mater. He taught at Harvard for 27 years. His contributions as a teacher, historian, investigator, theorist, administrator, statesman, and editor earned him a great deal of respect and recognition from his peers. By establishing the Boring Liberty Fund at Harvard, he received recognition from both students and faculty. He became known as "Mr. Psychology."

He was able to balance experimental psychology with philosophical science. His research was based on sensory and perceptual phenomena. He advocated for women in psychology and in military psychology.

He lived a life of integrity and sacrificed his own needs for those of his students. He encouraged students to learn to write better so their influence would be much more to the benefit of those who came late to read their works. He lived true to his Quaker upbringing.

He was the first historian of psychology. As a historian, he developed a course in the history of psychology that was held three times weekly for two hours over two years. It was a 200-lecture course. He loved the history of psychology. He wanted his students to love it likewise. The course was a crown jewel at Cornell. Once it was completed, he moved to Harvard and taught there for the next 27 years and to the end of his career.

His research on the moon and why it appears to have different sizes at different locations was his major accomplishment.

Additional reading: Boring, E., *Review of General Psychology*, 2002.

PRACTIAL ADVICE

If you want to truly understand something, try to change it.

Kurt Tsadek Lewin

Kurt Lewin (1890–1947) was born in Poland to German parents. He proposed the field theory of behavior, which held that behavior is the result of the individual and the environment. This included the study of personality, interpersonal conflict, and situational factors. It is the interaction between the two. Topological psychology was also his innovation. Much research originated from his theory.

Leadership style was a major area of study. He identified the autocratic leader, the Democratic leader, and the delegation leader. It was the democratic leader who served best in social situations. They were more likely to engage others, communicate with others, and seek the input of others.

Delegative leaders were prone to being laissez-faire, and autocratic leaders tended to be dictatorial and expected obedience.

He was often referred to as the "father of social psychology."

Additional reading: Lewin, K., *Principles of Topological Psychology*, McGraw-Hill, 1936.

WE LIVE BY PERCEPTION

The whole is greater than the sum of its parts.

Fritz Perls

Who said it? Dr. Perls (1893–1970) was the originator of what became known as Gestalt psychology. It is based on perception. Perception is always greater than the actual object or event that is being viewed at any given time. We introduce emotions, past experiences, motivation, attitudes, and values into every individual's perception. Thereby, the perceptual experience at any moment is what we additionally contribute to the perceptual event and what we learn or remember from it. We can best summarize the essence of perception in his phrase, "The whole is greater than the sum of its parts."

In Gestalt psychology, it is encouraged to consider all the factors that enter a given perceptional experience. Besides the object being perceived, there is an active interpretation of that perception on which it is based. This includes motivational factors, emotional factors, value-based factors, experiences, and so on. Hence, the idea of Gestalt psychology is the experience that when you look at something, the whole is greater than just the item or the sum of the items and parts that comprise the observation. One must consider all the factors that come into play to make up a complete observational experience.

Perception has always been the same throughout history. We understand it better these days, thanks to Gestalt psychology. It is important that we give recognition when we come to understand something or pursue something that we look at in the context of what we also bring to and contribute to the perceptual experience at the time from our past.

Essentially, the present is not independent of the past. Every experience is a combination of both. By applying Gestalt principles, we can better understand the nature of prejudice, bias, and personal opinion, for example.

Additional reading: Perls, F., *The Gestalt Approach and Eyewitness to Therapy*, The Gestalt Journal Press, 1992.

THE POWER OF A CHILD

What a child can do in cooperation today,
he can do alone tomorrow.

Lev Vygotsky

Who said it? Lev Vygotsky (1896–1934), a Russian and Soviet psychologist, was best known for his work on the psychological and cognitive development of children. He based his analysis on cultural-historical activity theory. The theory held that the social interactions of a child shape one's cognitive development and learning ability. Learning, he held, is a crucial social process as opposed to an independent journey of cognitive discovery.

We are born with four elementary mental functions: attention, sensation, perception, and memory. It is our social and cultural environment that allows us to use these elementary skills to develop and finally gain "higher mental functions." Essentially, peers, teachers, and parents provide the essential social interaction for learning to take place. Much of his thinking was similar to that of Piaget. Piaget focused on the environment with which the child interacts, but for Vygotsky, it was the social and cultural forces impacting the child during the formative years.

Some of these forces are innate, while others require parents, teachers, and others to specifically program them for the child. It is a process of becoming. We not only let the culture have its influence, but we also put a child in the right place and at the right time so that the culture will have its impact. The parent is the most critical influence of all people in this process for the child.

Dr. Vygotsky died prematurely from tuberculosis at age 39. He was honored at his funeral by being called the "Mozart of Psychology." He had many followers and students of his teachings who, after his death, wrote commentaries on his theory and teachings. We know mostly about the work of Vygotsky because of his students.

He was considered a seminal thinker. Many of his ideas and works continue to be explored today. The Communist Party of Russia followed and criticized his professional work, making his writings largely accessible to the western world. Died prematurely at age 38.

Additional reading: Vygoysky, L., *Mind in Society,* Harvard University Press, 1978.

WE LEARN FROM OUR CHILDREN

Learning is active; the mind is always evolving; the intellect is constantly developing; and finally, it reaches equilibrium.

Jean Paget

Who said it? Dr. Paget (1896–1980) grew up in Switzerland, became highly interested in the natural world, and wrote his first scientific paper at age 11. He studied the natural sciences. He became the director of the Jean-Jacques Rousseau Institute in Geneva. Much of his research was based on his own three children and their cognitive development. He received many honorary degrees and much international recognition. His primary research was conducted during the early 1900s. He followed in the footsteps of Freud and gained attention throughout America because of it.

Dr. Paget was a precocious young biologist who became fascinated with epistemology. As a result, he carved out his own understanding of a new discipline called genetic epistemology. It was a study of how intelligence changes as children grow. He was interested in the natural development of mental skills over time. He focused on the types, experiences, and quantities of children's learning.

Child development is primarily seen in the context of environmental factors. He focused on age-defined developmental stages. Essentially, children are active and autonomous learners, using their senses to interact with the world as they move through the developmental stages. Nurture was seen as the guide, giving children the freedom to experiment and explore on their own. It is a trial-and-error method of learning for children. Therefore, a good teacher simply supports children on their journey through these stages, constantly encouraging their creativity and imagination.

The goal of education is to create many adults who can do new things. His studies led him to conclude that learning is always active, involves an evolving mind, is constantly developing systematically through four stages, and finally reaches equilibrium. He spoke often about education and its impact on development. He was very interested in moral education.

Additional reading: Paget, J., *The Psychology of the Child*, Basic Books, 1962.

SOCIAL PERCEPTION

Give a thimble of dramatic facts, and we will rush to make generalizations as big as a tub.

Gordon Allport

Who said it? Gordon Allport (1897–1967) was a mild-mannered, diligent man with plain features. He had many research interests, among them prejudice, communication, and values, but personality, and in particular trait theory, was the central concern of his life. Allport was the youngest of four sons of a country doctor in Indiana. The family hails from England, and his mother is from Germany. Allport claims that his family was characterized by straightforward Protestant piety and hard work. He worked in his father's medical office, which was located in his home, washing bottles, caring for patients, tending the office, and so on. His father was known for his humanitarian values. He soon came to absorb his father's humanitarian outlook and values. He quoted his father's lifestyle by saying, "If every person worked as hard as he could and took only the minimum financial return required by his family needs, then there would be just enough wealth to go around."

As he grew older, volunteer work in social services became a defining aspect of his life. He had a deep-seated need to help people with problems. It gave him a feeling of confidence to offset a generalized inferiority feeling. His true interest in psychology and social service merged when he became convinced that to do effective social service, one needed a sound conceptualization of human personality.

Allport had many research interests, such as prejudice, communication, and values, but personality, and in particular trait theory, was of central concern to him. The father's favorite dictum was, "If every person worked as hard as he could and took only the minimum financial return required by his family's needs, then there would be just enough wealth to go around."

He wrote, "Social psychology is an attempt to understand and explain how thoughts, feelings, and the behavior of individuals are influenced by the actual, imagined, or implied presence of others." Over the years, social psychology has long been constructing theories about how our interactions with others affect our mental health and, conversely, how our mental processes and personalities affect our social behavior. Although Allport modified his theory of personality over the years, he always considered traits to be the fundamental and stable unit of personality.

He and his psychologist brother, Floyd, teamed up to develop a personality questionnaire to measure ascendant submission. They designed several situations and assessed whether a person would deal with them in an ascendant or submissive manner. After trying the test on several volunteers, they concluded that people who gave either an ascendant or submissive answer to any one challenging situation were highly likely to give the same kind of answer in other situations. They wrote, "People by and large do tend consistently to occupy a given spot on a continuum from high ascendants to a low of submission."

To demonstrate his devotion to detail, he and his brother counted all the words in the dictionary that designated distinctive kinds of human behavioral qualities. The total was about 18,000. They then divided those terms into various sub-categories. It came down to about 41 topics having significance in describing traits or manifestations of personality.

It came down to his study of personality, in which he reviewed individuals' personal documents and histories, their answers to questions in an interview, ratings by others, a questionnaire administered having to do with personality traits, both objective and projective tests, and observing individuals perform actual tasks assigned to them.

Over the years, he modified his views on personality but always considered traits to be the fundamental and stable unit of personality. Psychologists still regard personality psychology as all but simultaneous with the study of traits. His book, The Nature of Prejudice, is well used and the basis of many psychology classes in social psychology.

He saw social psychology as an effort to comprehend and explain how the actual, imagined, or implied presence of others affects people's thoughts, feelings, and behaviors. He gave credit to Plato, Aristotle, and Hobbs for having social psychology interests and drew upon social psychology concepts to explain political and philosophical ideas. He remained interested in the conscience aspect of man rather than the depths of the unconscious. Based on that, Allport was known to devote a good deal of his time to volunteer work and social services. He said it gave him a feeling of competence. He went on to say that to do effective social service, one needed a sound conception of human personality.

He had a great influence on another famous social psychologist, Muzafer Sherif, who studied the influence of other people on social judgment, not on one's performance. In contrast, he and Freud had a meeting on one occasion, which profoundly affected him. This came about by Allport asserting himself, contacting Freud, and letting him know he was going to be in Havana and wanted to meet with him. This meeting had profound effects on Alport. Allport was also disenchanted with behaviorism. He said that behaviorism portrayed the human being as purely a reactive organism, acting only in response to external prodding when, in fact, human beings are "proactive" and driven largely by their own goals, purposes, intentions, plans, and moral values. Such personality traits tend to define the behavior patterns and lifestyles of individuals.

Allport, G. *Personality: A Psychological Interpretation*, 1937.

SELF-CONTROL IS UTMOST

Love, work, and knowledge are the wellsprings of our lives; they should also govern them.

Wilhelm Reich

Who said it? Wilhelm Reich (1897–1957) was a psychoanalyst and a member of the second generation of analytic thinkers in psychology and psychiatry.

He was born in Ukraine. He died while in jail as a prisoner. He was accused of quackery and of being the leader of a sex cult. He was considered a foreigner and undesirable. He was selling accumulators, and he was subsequently arrested and imprisoned in 1956 for breaking the injunction.

He developed a system of psychoanalysis that concentrated on overall character structure rather than on individual neurotic symptoms.

He believed that contraceptives should be available to everyone, that childhood sexuality should be affirmed, and that sexual relationships between unmarried young adults were healthy. He also advocated for the legalization of abortion.

In later years, he moved away from psychoanalysis and directed his attention to Marxism. In 1928, he joined the communist party and toured the Soviet Union. There, he visited nursery schools and educational centers.

He further advocated the acceptance of sexuality and body work, through which he promoted full healing treatment, which would then improve a client's breathing, emotions, wounds, acceptance, and physical self, as well as communication patterns. Sexual repression was thought to ultimately seek expression in the muscles and organs, in the form of illness or impairment.

He advanced what is known as the "Tree of Life Orgone Pyramid." It was a tree of life with a spiritual meaning. Its branches stretched into the sky and its roots deep into the ground, and the tree of life represents the connection between heaven and earth and between eternal life, which reflect and symbolize the many aspects of life.

He also advanced full-body breathing, which involves individuals inhaling as deeply as possible and then fully exhaling. The therapist encourages the individual and treatment to be as free as possible while performing full-body breathing, making many sounds and movements that come forth during the session.

The tree of life was a metaphor to tell stories about one's life. Each part of the tree represents something about their life.

His writings influenced generations of intellectuals. He coined the phrase "the sexual revolution." His work over the years was trying to reconcile psychoanalysis with Marxism. He wanted to prevent neurosis rather than treat it. His emphasis was on Orgon therapy, which was used to treat cancer. He claimed a positive success rate. It was later determined to be fraud of the first magnitude. He did not adhere to the injunction to stop such therapy, so he was later arrested and imprisoned. Six tons of his publications on Oregon therapy were burned by order of the court. After a year in prison, he died. His contributions and his part of the story of the history of psychology are embarrassing.

Additional reading: Reich, W., *Listen, Little Man!*, Orgone Institute Press, 1948.

OUR THINKING OPENS THE GATE OF SUCCESS

Sooner or later, those who win are those who think they can.

Paul Tournie

Who said it? Dr. Tournie (1898–1986) was a Swiss physician. He conducted his personal counseling practice throughout the early years of the 1900s. He died in 1986. He became world-famous as a distinguished Christian physician. His ideas had a significant impact on the spiritual and psychosocial components of his patients' treatment and care. He was considered the most famous 20th-century Christian physician.

He was also a prolific author. His book, *The Meaning of Persons,* was his best-known work of the 50 books he wrote over his years of practice.

His aunt and uncle raised him as an orphan. He withdrew into himself and became lonely, shy, and depressed. Throughout his adolescence, he maintained a sense of insecurity, which he would hide behind an intellectual façade accentuated by his mathematical success in grade school and his knowledge of Greek. He lived a happy and fulfilled life. He experienced much pain, however, in the loss of his first wife. He died at age 88 due to carcinoma.

He was the pioneer of person-centered psychotherapy. He held that psychotherapy should have a spiritual dimension. Each person was to be seen in his or her own uniqueness and individuality. Therapy was to be the way a patient came to know himself and his uniqueness. Psychotherapy cannot be personal enough, he maintained. He provided therapy with the sense that a person could be whole even in a broken world.

The spiritual being in man was most intriguing to Dr. Tournie. While man is body and mind, the spiritual component is most important and influential in determining a person's lifestyle, actions, and being.

Tournie, through his writings and lectures, had a profound influence on the Christian community in the way the Christian believer thinks, talks, worships, and lives.

His writings, speaking, and therapy were based on his religious view of man and the distinction between the person and the personage.

Additional reading: Tournie, P., *The Meaning of Persons*, Harpers Collins, 1954.

THE FULLNESS OF OUR BRAIN

There seems to be a functional separation between the left and right sides of the brain: the left is more involved in verbal working memory, while the right is more active in spatial working memory.

Karl Lashley

Who said it? An American neurologist and psychologist, Karl Lashley (1898–1958), established the neurological research laboratories at the University of Minnesota and the University of Chicago. He taught classes at these two universities as well. Students came from all over the world to study with Lashley and joined the host of scholars who went on and subsequently identified specific brain functions and structures. The areas of study on learning and memory were also advanced by him and his students.

The research by Lashley was monumental. He was the first to empirically demonstrate the two hemispheres of the brain and how they functioned differently from each other. This observation was ground-breaking for much neurological research to follow. Since then, we have been able to specify areas of the brain and their relative importance for our overall functioning.

Further, it was Lashley who discovered that the brain functions as a mass action in accordance with the mutual functions of equipotentiality. That is, the brain functions as a whole as well as in parts, with one part capable of fulfilling the functions of another part of the brain.

John Watson mentored him. He was so influenced that he included behaviorism in his research and understanding of the brain.

Additional reading: Lashley, K., *Studies in the Dynamics of Behavior*, University of Chicago Press, 1932.

THE POWER OF LOVE

Love cures people—both the ones who give it and the ones who receive it.

Karl A. Menninger

Who said it? Karl Menninger (1893–1990), a graduate of Harvard, is well-known for his clinics and hospitals in Kansas as well as the East Coast. He successfully took on some exceedingly difficult assignments in treating people with serious mental illnesses. He was a spokesperson for psychology and psychiatry and their role in the treatment of mental illness. He actively practiced and managed his clinics during the 1900s.

To be sure, cure is possible, but it depends on love, he believed. One cannot give love until one receives it. One must learn how to accept love and how to give love. But once we learn how to receive and give love, we can experience the cure, whether it is depression, psychosis, anxiety, trauma, bipolar disorders, and so on.

Love is the basic commodity of life. Every child must experience unconditional love to grow, mature, and be healthy, as well as to be fully alive and experience life fully. Without love, there is the absence of growth and the absence of hope. He also drew strongly on forgiveness. Love and forgiveness were the primary acts of personal growth.

As Dr. Menninger said, "It all begins with love." That is the primary role of the parent, the grandparents, and those within the life experience and life circle of a young child. That love continues to follow the child, embrace the child, and engulf the child as the child matures, increases in age and experience, and becomes part of general society.

He is one of the therapists who grappled with the concept of sin. He developed a definition and wrote about how it plays a role in our lives, especially our emotional lives. Rogers followed him, Tournie, and others as sin was increasingly recognized as a real component of one's life and behavior patterns.

Additional reading: Menninger, K., *What Ever Became of Sin?* Hawthorn Books, 1973.

THE HEALING PROCESS WITHIN US

I am always looking outside myself for confidence, but it comes from within. It is there all the time.

Anna Freud

Who said it? Anna Freud (1895–1982) was a British psychoanalyst born in Vienna, the sixth and youngest child of Sigmund Freud and Marth Bernays. She actively practiced psychiatry in Australia.

She emphasized the importance of the ego and its defensive mechanisms, helping to elucidate how children's emotional conflicts influence their development. Her book, entitled *The Ego and the Mechanism of Defense,* was one of her major contributions.

She promoted parent guidance and school consultation as essential functions of every practicing child therapist. She spent her life with children. She was not particularly socially outgoing or involved in the social world of her day otherwise. She did not enjoy the social world as much as her father did.

Her work primarily focused on the development and description of various mechanisms of one's emotional defense system. The defense strategies used by people include repression, projection, and regression, to name a few. We became skilled in the use of such defenses by her patients over time as they were successfully employed to defend one's own ego or personal self.

As a child, she was very jealous of her older sister's beauty and did not have a positive relationship with her mother. Her father, Sigmund, once said, "Anna has become downright beautiful through naughtiness." She never completed a medical or psychological degree. She learned most of her work through her contacts with her father. When Sigmund became a cancer patient, she devoted her primary time to his care. She often represented her father on various occasions, including various ceremonies where he was recognized or honored.

In 1938, when the Nazis invaded Austria, she and her family moved to London. Her father died shortly thereafter. She went on to establish a child-analytic practice in London. There, she also provided foster care to children during the war. These were child nurseries. She capitalized on it and observed the impact of the separation of children from their families. She noted how such separation affects children relative to their normal development. She wrote extensively about children's daily development. She subsequently published these papers after the war. She then moved to Australia and practiced psychotherapy there until her death in 1982. She was far from living in her father's shadow. She made many contributions of her own, including child psychoanalysis and the defense mechanism to preserve the ego.

She had a social service side to her. She began working with and analyzing children from socially and economically disadvantaged backgrounds and was committed to sharing her analytic work with those who work with such children, such as parents, teachers, and pediatricians. At one point, she came to the United States and taught briefly at Yale Law School, where she applied her psychoanalytic ideas to family and crime.

Additional reading: Freud, A., *The Ego and the Mechanism of Defense*, International Universities Press, 1936.

HISTORICAL CONTRIBUTIONS IN PSYCHOLOGY

1900 - 1950

WE ARE OUR OWN FRAME OF REFERENCE

The more you know yourself, the more patience you have for what you see in others.

Erik Erikson

Who said it? Erik Erikson (1902–1994) was a Danish, German, and American child psychoanalyst who was devoted to the study of child development. He started to study psychology at Harvard for the Ph.D. degree but was at odds with the program's focus on quantitative psychology and science. He dropped out of the program. For the next 20 years, he practiced psychoanalysis, taught, and conducted his research at Berkley and Yale.

He modified some of the thinking of Freud and placed his emphasis more on the person's ongoing and current life experience. He held that it was more of the current and/or present life factors that determined the behavior and problems in a person's life than historic events and influences, as Freud and others emphasized.

As we understand ourselves, we come to understand other people better. Historical factors come later in the pursuit of knowing oneself and others.

When we come to understand ourselves, we are more tolerant of others. One's daily experience was considered the place to start. We are always more patient and kinder towards others when we understand ourselves. To be an effective person, one must know themselves first and foremost. This comes through self-study and how we form our relationships with others. We become more fully human as we know ourselves better.

While we understand the idea of knowing ourselves and then getting to know others much better, it is still important to realize and understand ourselves first and then understand the world in which we live. Then, we can proceed to understand the people with whom we live and willingly open up and share our lives with them. Each of us has social significance. Each of us has also had our traumas and cultural accomplishments. Through these events, we come to see ourselves for who we are. Over time, we experience identity, growth, and a life cycle of experiences, all of which impact and shape us.

The pursuit of oneself is made possible through the process of psychotherapy as well as other pursuits. By being willing to share ourselves with others, we learn more about ourselves and about the lives of others. Opening up and talking is the first step. Talking about yourself is the second step. Sharing experiences with others is the third step. Asking questions is a good fourth step. It goes on from there. In all, he wrote sixty-four books.

He held the position that our ego constantly changes due to our social interactions and the new information we acquire from the gleam of others.

He took the position that personality development occurs in eight stages and that each stage's outcome profoundly affects the development of our personality.

The eight stages of human development he proposed are:

Trust vs. Mistrust

Autonomy vs. Shame and Doubt

Initiative vs. Guilt

Industry vs. Inferiority

Identity vs. Role Confusion

Intimacy vs. Isolation

Generativity vs. Stagnation

Integrity vs. Despair

His theory focused much on the early stages of life. If one feels fulfilled in each stage of life, peace and a meaningful life and career will result. He was one of many who speculated on the human growth and development process and how it shapes our lives as adults.

Additional reading: Erickson, E., *Childhood and Society*, W.W. Norton, 1950.

OPTIMISM

When I look at the world, I'm pessimistic, but
when I look at People, I'm optimistic.

Carl Rogers

Who said it? Pessimism and optimism are critical values or ways of life for any individual. It's a choice, according to Carl Rogers (1902–1987), the founder of humanistic psychology. People become what they believe and how they believe, think, and talk. Optimism is the operative way of life for Carl Rogers. To think positively, optimistically, futuristically, and hopefully is the optimum way to live, he believed.

Others have added a theme to the concept of optimism using the term "cautious optimism." It is good to be optimistic, but not to be grandiose or to overstate one's hope. One must be realistic and cautious. Even optimism should be moderate.

Yes, optimism and pessimism are even with us today. We all struggle with the dualistic nature of life—to be optimistic or pessimistic, to be more optimistic or less pessimistic. We learn optimism. We depreciate ourselves and our situation in life through pessimistic thinking. It only acts to deny us a life of joy and fulfillment. Becoming optimistic is a learning process—yes, even a life-long learning process. Engaging in therapy is an effective way to learn to become more optimistic and less pessimistic. We are all better people as we adopt an optimistic lifestyle and way of relating to others. Rogers would want us all to think and relate optimistically as we go about our daily affairs.

Rogers' style of therapy is well known. He rephrased the patient's statements and asked if that was what was said or meant. He wanted patients to feel they were listened to and understood. He was a caring person and a therapist. His style of therapy was congruent with his caring personality.

Additional reading: Rogers, C., *On Becoming a Person: The Therapist's View of Psychotherapy*, Houghton Mifflin, 1961.

TRUE EDUCATION

Education is what survives when what has been learned has been forgotten.

B.F. Skinner

Who said it? Harvard University was privileged to have B.F. Skinner (1904–1990) as one of its prime faculty members in psychology during the early 1900s. H was profoundly influenced by historical figures such as Pavlov, James, Darwin, and others. In contrast, his work profoundly influenced others, such as Rotter, Homans, and many others.

His work had the greatest influence on modern education today by focusing on the process of learning how to learn. Skinner worked with pigeons to figure out how learning takes place. He was able to teach pigeons to navigate a missile and live life based on a reinforcement system. That made him famous. He profoundly influenced how we learn and how teaching is to be most effectively carried out and conducted.

His statement, as noted above, is profound. Skinner did not emphasize facts or a base of knowledge, although those were important to him. What he did emphasize was the process of learning how to learn. It was he who developed the learning theory that we learn the behavior patterns that are reinforced or rewarded and forget or extinguish those behavior patterns that are non-reinforced or even punished. It is not what we know; it is how we came to know and how we came to behave in a consistent and forward-focused manner in making behavioral choices and surviving in your daily environment.

There were three basic principles by which we learn: reinforcement theory, extinction theory, and punishment theory. These are the three mechanisms that are operative in a person's life, shaping his behavior patterns to be less maladaptive and more adaptive and goal-oriented.

Skinner struck it right. Reinforcement of any behavior pattern strengthens that behavior pattern and influences a person to do it more regularly, frequently, and consistently, whether that behavior is considered to be good or bad, adaptive or maladaptive, or wanted or unwanted. It relates to all behavior, not just academic learning. To change behavior, you either punish it or extinguish it by following it with non-reinforcement.

Learning is never over. It continues well after school has been dismissed. Learning is an ongoing process. It is a lifestyle.

Additional reading: Skinner, B.F., *The Analysis of Behavior*, McGraw-Hill, 1961.

THE BRAIN COMES ALIVE

Neuron cells that fire together wire together. Use it or lose it.

Donald Hebb

Who said it? Donald Hebb (1904–1985) was a leading Canadian researcher in the latter half of the 1900s. Hebb was a psychologist who became interested in how the neurological system is the underpinning of behavior. He determined that behavior patterns create neurological patterns of activity. He espoused the concept of brain functions based on cells working together and forming "cell assemblies." Then they form "phase sequences," which are a series of cell assemblies. His students coined these phrases to summarize the research findings of Dr. Hebb, their professor, and a man with whom they became friendly.

Brain activity is complex, he said. Single cells bond with other cells and eventually form an assembly line of cells, which then makes the associated behavioral pattern more predictable and organized. Hebb advanced our understanding of brain functions to a much higher level than had been the case previously.

Brain cells were much better understood because of Hebb's conceptualization, as was brain functioning. His theory of the brain still holds true in part even today. Our basic understanding of the brain advanced under Hebb. The problem of understanding behavior is based on our level of understanding of the total action of the nervous system at the time.

Hebb applied his work to the fields of psychology, education, and neurology. In time, he became known as one of the leading scientists in the study of the brain and its relationship to spatial learning and associated behavior.

Due to the strong influence of Dr. Hebb, psychology quickly became a neurological and behavioral scientific pursuit. He was obsessed with the relationship between the brain and behavior. He held that without understanding the neurological structures and functions of the brain, we cannot fully understand why people do what they do. This is what psychology is all about, anyway. The future will be even more so, he predicted.

Further, Hebb viewed motivation and learning as related properties. He believed that everything in the brain was inner-related and worked together. His theory was that everything we experience in our environment is a set of cell assemblies. This cell assembly network is essentially the brain's thoughts and ideas. Following formation, stimulation from the environment can activate the phase sequences. The more stimulating and richer the environment, the more the cell assemblies and phase sequences grow and learn.

This research led him to the belief that the environment was very important to learning for children. Children learn by building up these cell assemblies and phase sequences, and a rich environment with varied opportunities for sensory and motor experiences contributes to a child's development of cell assemblies and phase sequences necessary for long-term functioning in the adult years.

He and his daughter raised rats in their home, like a home laboratory, to assess his theory. He found that raising these animals in an enriched environment improved maze learning in adulthood. His work contributed to the development of the Head Start program, which is still used today. Hebb started his own preschool program for low-income families. He held that children are prepared for school through early learning in a cognitively stimulating educational environment.

In a study in which he tracked 42 children over time, he found that two of the most important aspects of language acquisition are the economic advantages of the children and the frequency of language experiences. That is, children from lower-income homes learn fewer words and acquire vocabulary more slowly than children of professional parents with higher economic status. He believed that children should be evaluated on their ability to think and create rather than their ability to memorize and reprocess older ideas.

Dr. Hebb's work is true today as well. We are still studying and trying to understand the relationship between brain functions and behavioral patterns. This is and will be an ongoing area of pursuit, with considerable interest and insightful findings as we go forward. Already, the work of Hebb and others has contributed to our understanding of and treatment of significant medical problems, such as Parkinson's disease and other neuro-medical and neuro-behavioral problems people experience.

Additional reading: Hebb, D., *The Organization of Behavior*, Science Editions, 1949.

COMFORT CARE IS A BASIC NEED

The infant and young child should experience a warm, intimate, and continuous relationship with their mother in which both find satisfaction and enjoyment, and not doing so might have significant and irreversible mental health consequences.

Harry Harlow

Who said it? Dr. Harlow (1905–1981) practiced and taught as an experimental psychologist at the University of Wisconsin. He was a determined and endless stream of energy. He demanded much of himself and of his graduate students. He was known to appear at his laboratory at any time of the day or night, and he expected to see his graduate students there engaged in some type of research project.

He primarily studied the relationship between monkeys during their infancy and a mother object, which fulfilled their need for food. He placed monkeys in cages with surrogate mothers made of wire with a feeding bottle attached. Another monkey was made of soft, cuddly terry cloth with no bottle attached. It was thought that the baby monkey would remain with the mother, who provided food. However, it was found that the monkeys spent most of their time with the cloth mother, viewing her as a secure base and clinging to her for safety when frightened objects were introduced into the cage. Later, after the infant monkeys were attached to the cloth mother and she was able to rock the infant and provide food, the attachment was even stronger. It was suggested then that the main function of nursing might be to ensure body contact with the mother. Even when a cloth mother was unable to provide nourishment, there was a strong attraction and attachment.

The work of Harlow was enormously important because it was understood in those days that parents needed to rock and pick up a crying infant and provide nourishment. The work of Harlow has strongly impacted and changed the focus of the approach to parenting throughout the world. He tried to explain why some children who are abused by a mother or are rejected by the mother live a life of rejection, detachment, and abandonment. It was the nature of physical contact that seemed to be more important than merely providing nourishment, whether that was in a healthy form or an unhealthy form of nourishment. In essence, infants become attached to their caregiver because the caregiver provides more warmth, protection, and care than nourishment.

This line of research disproved the theories of Freud, who based one's attachment to a caregiver on the provision of food and nourishment by that caregiver.

Harlow also held that contact comfort is essential to the psychological development and health of animals as well as children. Therefore, the main feature of nursing, for example, is to ensure the infant gets bodily contact and comfort from the mother.

He was also known for his infamous social isolation research on monkeys.

Additional reading: Harlow, H., *Learning to Love*, J. Aronson, *1974*.

MEASURING NATURAL INTELLIGENCE

Psychological assessment is based on quantification, rankings, and ratings.

Raymond Cattell

Who said it? Dr. Cattell (1905–1998) was born in England and first studied chemistry before turning to psychology in the early 1920s. His primary work was in the United States after 1937, teaching at Clark, Harvard, and the University of Illinois. He ended his career at the University of Hawaii in 1998. He served as president of the American Psychological Association in 1997.

He was often critically attacked for his views on intelligence. He believed that nations should safeguard high-inherited intelligence through eugenics. He developed the famous Culture-Faire Intelligence Test in 1940. It measured fluid intelligence through visually presented pattern-related problems that required no particular reading ability and no particular prior learning or knowledge to solve a problem. It was considered a good measure of intelligence cross-culturally. It was used with a fair degree of confidence.

He developed his views on intelligence when he was a student of Charles Sperman in Britain, who defined the g-factor of general intelligence that served as the foundation for all learning. The g-factor is made up of two components: fluid intelligence and crystalized intelligence. Together, we understand it as a general index of overall intelligence. One's vocabulary was thought to be a good index of the g-factor.

The g-factor was considered a general intelligence factor present at birth. Some might refer to this factor as our native intelligence and add to it with learned intelligence. It was considered stable and a good predictor of general verbal intelligence.

We need to appreciate our native abilities, and even more, we need to appreciate the intelligence we acquire through our experiences, making up our abilities and working intelligence. He was well-known for a 16-factor model of personality to which he devoted himself for most of his final years.

Additional reading: Cattell, R., *Intelligence*, McGraw-Hill, 1950.

ATTITUDE

Your attitude is what makes the difference.

Victor Frankl

Who said it? Dr. Frankl (1905–1997) was a psychiatrist well-known for his wartime experiences, for which he is counted as a survivor of the concentration camps where he spent many years of his adult life. Frankl was widely known for his time and experience in the German concentration camps.

This quote summarizes one of his observations while awaiting his release. He survived, he said, because of his attitude about his future and how to maximize his circumstances each day.

No matter what our circumstances, Dr. Frankl points out that we have one ultimate choice, and that is to determine our own personal attitudes about the situation we are in at the time. It was his belief that circumstances do not do us in, but the attitude we have about the circumstances is what will do us in or allow us to survive.

He observed that those who had the attitude or the belief that someday they would be freed and be able to escape were the ones that survived. Those who believed they would escape by some predetermined date did not survive. In other words, they had limited hope, and when that hope was not fulfilled, they gave up and died.

Situations in life come to us. We are to adapt readily and win over them. To do so, said Frankl, is to choose our attitude. By doing so, we either survive or fall prey to the events of life. He concluded that it was his attitude of openness, hope, and anticipation that contributed to his survival.

Frankl wrote and lectured about his experience and used it to teach how to survive and live through perilous situations in life.

He also held the view that "between stimulus and response, there is a space. In that space is our power to choose how to respond in whatever situation we are in at the moment." Frankl knew the experience of freedom more than anyone. He believed in and lectured on the old adage, "Don't count your chickens before they are hatched." "Tough times come to all." "Wait it out." "Your time of freedom will come." "Don't push it." "Live with hope and a prayer."

Additional reading: Frankl, V., *Man's Search for Meaning*, Beacon Press, 1946.

NO PERFECT PARENT

Parental deficiencies are seen as a vulnerability factor rather than a direct cause of later difficulties.

John Bowlby

Who said it? Dr. John Bowlby (1907–1990) focused his research attention on the effects of infants and young children being separated from their mothers during the formative years. Although the effect of the loss of the mother on the developing child had been considered earlier by Freud and other theorists, Bowlby's work on delinquent and affectionless children and children raised in institutional care facilities led him to be recognized worldwide. It was he who established the maternal deprivation hypothesis in 1951.

His work sparked significant debate and research on the issue and importance of children's early maternal relationships, or lack thereof. Many different therapists with various orientations conducted extensive research on his concept of maternal deprivation after that. This research led to a general understanding of the concept of "failure to thrive." Being deprived of maternal love and care results in a host of failures and impairments in all areas of life—social, emotional, intellectual, spiritual, and physical.

Further, he underscored that an ongoing relationship with the child is as important a part of parenting as the involvement of various family experiences, discipline, and childcare for a child. In other words, a parent and child cannot be too close during the growing years. A child needs to know without doubt about his acceptance by his parents as well as their love.

Bowlby was most interested in watching personality growth from birth onward and seeking those forces that shaped it. He tried to base his theory and ideas on first-hand evidence, which is different from what had been going on before, which was primarily theoretical in nature.

His studies of children raised in institutions found them deficient in emotional and personality development. He attributed that to the lack of maternal attachment. It was Bowlby who established the maternal deprivation hypothesis in 1951. The hypothesis states that children deprived of maternal care experience severe impairments in their physical development, cognitive functioning, and in all areas of their social and emotional lives.

Bowlby proposed his theory of attachment in four phases:

Pre-Attachment: Birth to six weeks

Attachment in the Making: Six to Seven Months

Clear–cut attachment: seven to twenty-four months.

Formation of a Reciprocal Relationship: Twenty-Four Months

He theorized that infants are genetically programmed to behave in certain ways, such as by crying, smiling, and cooing. That evokes care and, hence, survival. Further, the mother's nurture in facilitating gender attachment in the infant, at a sensitive period in the child's development, was highly important.

This special bond, which gives an infant a sense of security and identity, is crucial to normal personality development. Without it, he stated, "The child is likely to develop an affectionless character and to be permanently vulnerable to psychopathology." This finding led many to speculate on the cause of criminality and personality disorders, such as narcissism.

Bowlby's views also aroused great interest as well as discomfort for many Americans who were experiencing a rising divorce rate, as well as the feminine movement, with caused many women and mothers to work, leaving their children with caretakers in the 1960s and beyond.

Many child psychologists doubted that the sensitive period was that specific and crucial or that mothers were as all-important and irreplaceable as Bowlby seemed to indicate. But most of them agreed that, under certain normal circumstances, attachment to the mother or a mother substitute does occur and is a major force in personality development.

A series of studies by Bowlby with babies indicated that young children smile, giggle, and make a variety of sounds when a mother is actively engaged with the child. But when a mother turns away, babies immediately go blank and stop smiling. This is also true, but even more pronounced, when a child experiences prolonged social deprivation.

From these studies, he published his research in a book entitled *Secure Base: Clinical Applications of Attachment Theory,* 1988. It was well read and provided a basic understanding of the whole field of childhood attachment for children. In other research, he compared children raised under three different conditions: in a kibbutz, in their own family home, and those raised in a large house by professional caretakers. For example, he studied a variety of aspects of children, such as their smiling behavior. Over time, the smiling behavior of children was most positive in family-reared children and least positive in professional institutions reared by a professional caretaker.

Additional reading: Bowlby, J., *Separation Anxiety and Anger,* Basic Books, 1976.

FUTURISTIC THINKING

Depression is the inability to construct a future.

Rollo May

Who said it? Rollo May (1909–1994) was an offshoot of Freudian thinking and a mode of therapy. However, he emphasized more of a social and contemporary source of influence on a person's daily life and behavior pattern. He practiced as a therapist throughout the early and middle years of the 1900s. He is recognized as the father of existential psychology.

Rollo May put his finger on the pulse when it comes to depression. If one does not have a sense of the future, depression sets in. If one has a sense of the future based on some form of violence or catastrophic event, depression not only sets it but so does a great deal of fear, anger, and anxiety. A double whammy, to be sure.

However, when one cannot think of a future or be able to conceptualize a future, a sense of helplessness and hopelessness sets in. Helplessness is a very self-defeating and distressing form of depression. We live and thrive on our ability to see a future, work towards it, and attain it, at least in part. Having a sense of ability rather than disability is important as we view the future. However, it is important that our future be viewed as being within the realm of possibility so that it generates hopefulness, from which we thrive.

Depression has always been with us, and it always will be. The question is, "Who will be depressed?" In some way, we all experience depression at some point in our lives. Some for brief periods of time, and others for a prolonged period.

Since depression is always with us and always will be, it is most important to ask patients, particularly younger people, the question, "Where do you see yourself being five years from now?" If they give a pretty good answer or a very clear answer, the question can then be reframed by asking, "Where would you like to be ten years from now?" It gives a sense of whether the person has a future and can conceptualize a future. This also helps the therapist gauge a person's depression or likelihood of depression.

The message is true for all of us. What is your plan for the next five years? Ten years? Looking ahead is healthy and goal-motivating and attaining. Goals require plans. Through our plans, we attain the goal. Looking ahead is necessary and essential for success. Apathy and emptiness were the two malaises of his day. That occurs when people lose their purpose and direction in life. Psychotherapy helps people become more human, make better choices, and form communities. Effective psychotherapy stimulates relationship-building skills and the pursuit of learning opportunities.

Good choices lead to growth in freedom and responsibility. Psychotherapy is to set people free. Communication is how people come together and experience a healing community.

His book, *Love and Will,* is a good contribution to the understanding of morality. We must not miss the opportunity to understand the real meaning of love, the will, and their interrelationship. On this topic, he held that the opposite of love is not hate but apathy. It is love that motivates our highest achievement. He formulated four kinds of love: sexual, eros, philia, and agape. A blend of the four requires both self-assertion and the affirmation of another person.

Additional reading: May, R., *Man's Search for Himself*, W.W. Norton & Company, 2009.

WHAT ARE YOU?

If you plan on being anything less than you are capable of being, you will probably be unhappy all the days of your life.

Abraham Maslow

Who said it? Maslow (1909–1970) distinguished himself as a psychologist by providing guidance in the pursuit of what a person could fully become. He referred to this as the pursuit of self-actualization. Anything short of that was insufficient, unacceptable, and an indication that a person had fallen short of his potential.

For Maslow, becoming a psychologist was only possible by opposing the influence of his parents. He also defied tradition by marrying his cousin. That marriage resulted in the birth of two children.

Maslow, a professor of psychology at the University of Wisconsin and Columbia University, believed that man could develop to one's fullest capacity. Only then would he be happy and have a sense of fulfillment. It is to achieving one's purpose and meaning in life that represents self-actualization. We are not to stop short of complete personal fulfillment. If we do, happiness and contentment will never be fully experienced. Likewise, satisfaction in life cannot be fully experienced. Further, one's contribution to life and to the enhancement of others would not be fully experienced unless one was able to first achieve his own state of self-actualization.

Maslow was best known for his Hierarchy of Needs. We all start with the need for food and shelter. We then advance towards the ultimate need for self-actualization. Life is a progressive and systematic process of meeting our basic needs throughout life and striving for a higher order and level of functioning.

He also advocated for religion to be a legitimate subject of study and scientific investigation, as did many other mental health experts at the time. His book, *Religious Values and Peak Experiences,* is a classic in the study of religion and science.

Maslow disagreed that we go forward or backward just for the sake of safety. He advocated for the goal of achieving self-actualization. To live life fully and beyond one's comfort zone is the ultimate thing a person can do. Man is to search for the best and his unknown creative future. This is his primary task as he proceeds in his search for meaning. Growth is a process in the search for meaning. Self-actualization is the result to be realized.

The pursuit of self-actualization has always been the ultimate pursuit of man and always will be. We may not call it that, but we strive for complete fulfillment. We each have an unusual way to define this pursuit of fulfillment. It represents man's eternal pursuit of personal happiness and social stratification.

In the pursuit of self-actualization, we process through a series of steps or aspects of life. Maslow believed that self-actualization could not be reached until his basic physiological needs were met, his need for safety was achieved, his need for love and belonging was met, and his self-esteem was achieved. These basic needs were called deficiency needs.

Maslow was also of the belief that a higher set of needs were also essential to satisfy before self-actualization could be realized. They were called the growth needs. They included both cognitive and aesthetic needs. Growth was viewed as a progressive process in each of these need areas being met starting in the early years of life. He called this formula the Hierarchy of Needs.

Ultimately, Maslow held the position that man could only achieve self-transcendence by helping others and connecting with others or something outside of oneself. He held the basic belief that "what a man can be, he must be." In this statement, Maslow tosses out a challenge to all of us to live above our current circumstances and push ourselves a little. By so doing, we become more of a person and will live beyond our circumstances. It is that last push that make us excel and go a step beyond our current life experience as we know it.

Additional reading: Maslow, A., *Towards a Psychology of Being*, Wiley, 1962.

A DOUBLE MESSAGE

An effective marriage must have two components:
marital appreciation and marital appreciation.

Harlin Parker

Who said it? Dr. Parker (1910–1992) was a California psychiatrist in the mid-1900's and focused his clinical practice on the marriage of young couples and the medication management of patients. In the process of these counseling sessions, he developed his understanding of an effective marriage based on the concept of appreciation. At the time of his death, he was authoring a book on marriage appreciation. He had great delight in sharing his newly formed view of marriage. He saw all marriages alike in terms of appreciation. They just differed in the degree to which they experienced appreciation for each other and the degree to which the marriage appreciated in value over time.

An effective marriage has two aspects of marital appreciation. First, an effective marriage must demonstrate a strong appreciation for each other. There must be an appreciation for the couple's similarities, differences, skills, contributions, personalities, and family history, as well as their separate histories and educational levels. The appreciation list goes on and on.

Also, an effective marriage must manifest a second type of marital appreciation. The quality of the marriage itself must appreciate over time, improve over time, get better over time, have more value over time, and have more worth over time. Marriage must generate a greater value by itself for the general community. It must contribute value and significance to the community. The marriage must have an impact on the couple beyond the impact of the couple. Unfortunately, we often give less consideration to this second type of appreciation. Dr. Parker often thought of these as the "two faces of a marriage."

Marriages today are like they have always been. Some are rocky, some are dysfunctional, and some are disastrous. On the other hand, many flourish, thrive, and enjoy the long-term, ever-increasing richness of the relationship. Every marriage over time must experience an appreciation of value, worth, and acceptance for each other as unique individuals, while at the same time coming to appreciate the value of the relationship itself.

Note: Dr. Parker was not able to complete his book due to his sudden death.

SELF-CONTROL AND SELF-DEVELOPMENT

The best years of your life are the ones in which
you decide your problems are your own.
You do not blame them on your mother,
the ecology, or the president.
You realize that you control your own destiny.

Albert Ellis

Who said it? Albert Ellis (1913–2007) is a well-known psychologist of the 1900s who focused his therapeutic approach on identifying the irrational beliefs of an individual and changing those irrational beliefs to become more rational. A second area of interest was that of becoming more self-controlled and self-managed. He encouraged an internal locus of control as compared to an external locus of control. People who have an internal locus of control are happier, healthier, and more motivated to make improvements in their lives. The combination of these two changes in the life of an individual was the answer to many of the life problems people experience.

Ellis emphasized what is known as rational-emotive behavioral therapy. This was a type of cognitive-behavioral therapy that helped individuals change their irrational beliefs to become rational. It also helped people see the events of their lives as being under their own personal control. He challenged people who believed that the life events that happened to them were a result of fate, luck, chance, or the actions of powerful others in their lives. He emphasized taking personal responsibility. It was a matter of changing irrational thinking to become rational. It was a matter of taking charge of how one responds to circumstances and situations in life.

Here are a few examples of irrational thinking:

- *For me to feel loved or accepted by almost everyone as an adult human, it is absolutely necessary.*

- *I must be competent in everything, or I will never succeed.*
- *My emotions are outside of my control.*
- *I can never make a mistake, or I will be seen as a failure.*

For Ellis, life is 10% what happens to us and 90% how we react to it. As a result, people who developed this self-directed manner of living and thought rationally became healthier, happier, and felt more personally in control and powerful.

This concept of personal control is as true today as it was in the day of Ellis. Indeed, we all have the choice of blaming others or depending on others and circumstances to change so we can live life better. In contrast, Ellis was a strong spokesperson for personal responsibility, personal choice, and determining one's own personal destiny so that life could be lived better.

Additional reading: Ellis, A., *A Guide to Rational Living*, Wilshire Book Company, 1975.

FEARLESS LIVING

You can live life without fear.

Joseph Wolpe

Who said it? Dr. Wolpe (1915–1997), while being a psychiatrist, advanced psychology more than most psychologists. His area of influence was the advancement of behavior therapy and the use of systematic desensitization to treat anxiety-based disorders. Interestingly, he took no psychology course in college or medical school. His medical training was received in South Africa. He taught, served as a therapist, and mentored psychologists at the Eastern Pennsylvania Psychiatric Institute. He was recognized on numerous occasions for his contributions by various psychological groups.

Wolpe's approach to therapy came from WWII, when he noted that the traditional approaches to therapy were of little value. He brought new life into the field of therapy at a time when behavior therapy was becoming a strong option for patients who had little success with traditional psychotherapy.

He was known for the use of exposure therapy, reciprocal inhibition, and assertiveness. Students came from all over to study under him and learn the methods he utilized with positive results.

He was a leader in the establishment of journal publications devoted to behavior therapy. The field of behavior therapy advanced due to his leadership.

Additional reading: Wolpe, J., *The Practice of Behavior Therapy*, Pergamon Press, 1982.

HOW WE BECOME THE PERSON WE ARE

Critical life events shape life.

Julian Rotter

Who said it? Dr. Rotter (1916–1987) taught at Ohio State University. He was both a psychotherapist and an experimentalist. As a therapist, he was a behaviorist, which gave him respect for cognitive processes and emotions. Rotter found that his patient's basic attitude was that life is formed by critical experiences, some good and others bad.

He theorized that when particular acts were either rewarded or not rewarded, people developed generalized expectations about which kinds of circumstances and behaviors would or would not be rewarded in the future. For example, a student who studies diligently, gets good grades, wins praise, and feels good about himself may come to expect that challenging work in other situations will be similarly rewarding. In contrast, a student who studies hard but fails to get good grades and is not rewarded may come to expect that, in general, hard work does not pay off. Rotter's studies eventually came to be known as "locus of control theory." That eventually led to an understanding of what we came to know as "learned helplessness."

Rotter and his colleagues eventually developed a personality test known as the Internal/External Locus of Control Scale. It is made up of twenty-nine questions. The results would indicate if one felt he had little control over events in his life as compared to those who felt in charge of their own lives.

People who score at one end of the continuum on the external locus of control scale tend to attribute their successes to powerful others, such as physicians, attorneys, and ministers. A mid-range score indicates a belief in fate, luck, or chance as a determinant of things that happen to them. In contrast, people who score at the other end of the continuum attribute their successes and failures to their own intelligence, level of work produced, personal diligence, and other personal traits.

Much research has been conducted using the LOC scale. For example, studies have found that internals are less likely than externals to sympathize with people in need of help since internals believe that needy people brought their troubles on themselves.

In another study, internals feel proud when they succeed but feel ashamed or guilty when they fail. In contrast, externals feel less strongly about either success or failure. It was felt that normal, healthy individuals strike a balance between internal and external. The phrase that identifies the differences is, "I caused the good things (internal)," but "the bad things were forced upon me" (external)." Further, chance, fate, and luck are always an excuse or explanation for the outcome of an event.

The test developed by Rotter and his colleague, Dr. James, has been widely used in clinical and forensic situations to assess how one will act in a future situation or explain why people behaved as they did under a particular situation occurring in their life at the time.

Further, the test has been helpful in our understanding of how pain patients deal with their chronic pain.

Overall, the LOC test has been well regarded in the clinical community of psychologists.

Additional reading: Rotter, J., *Personality and Social Psychology*, Routledge, 2013.

The Place of Dialogue

Tact and diplomacy are fine in international relations, in politics, and perhaps even in business. In science, only one thing matters, and that is the fact.

Hanz Eysenck

Who said it? Dr. Eysenck (1916–1997) was a British psychologist specializing in personality traits and related behavioral styles. He is best known for his formulation of introversion, extraversion, and neuroticism (anxiety). He traced how these traits function differently in our daily lives. Individual differences were very important to Eysenck. He studied them systematically and extensively. He was actively involved in his research on this topic during the early and mid-tears of the 1960s. Due to his fear of flying, he rarely traveled outside of England.

Eysenck held a strong view of psychology as a science. It was important to him that those who seek the advice of a psychologist can be assured that the advice they are getting is based on scientific research. However, facts and truth are always seen in the context of probability. There are no absolutes, according to Eysenck. Instead, we tend to say, "It is more probable than not," or we might express it as, "Within the realm of probability . . ."

Yes, science is a relevant force and way of understanding ourselves, each other, our world, as well as our environment. All of these operate within the sense of scientific thought and data. This means that there are no absolutes. No one can speak for certain. We speculate. We conceptualize. We think theoretically. We organize our thoughts on a topic around some central theme, and we create theories about how things operate and how things exist. Then, our theories and concepts are put to the test and validated or not.

To be sure, the scientific world is a vastly different world from the political world. In politics, we have great freedom to speculate, pontificate, and conjecture as we put forth our thoughts in terms that would be considered more absolute or definite.

For Eysenck, the force of a statement by a national figure, whether it be political, religious, scientific, governmental, or whatever, should be taken as the gospel truth or absolute truth. It is through dialogue and interaction with others of different streams of thought that we develop understanding and relate to our world and to each other as accurately and effectively as possible.

Further, we need to associate with those who have a different viewpoint or way of life. In so doing, we experience growth, learn how to live in a diverse society, and do so successfully. The basic skills to do so are assertive communication and feeling comfortable being with those of a different faith or way of life. Living within one's comfort zone is living a plastic life, not a happy, creative, or meaningful life.

Additional reading: Eysenck, H., *Rebel with a Cause*, Transaction Publication, 1997.

HOW DO WE COMMUNICATE?

If we know one language, we can learn another.

Charles Osgood

Who said it? Dr. Osgood (1916–1991) was a long-term professor of psychology at the University of Illinois. His focus was on communication styles and formats. He held that our communication pattern is circular and not linear. He was known to submit himself to his own research to get a feel for what the research subject would experience. Much of his research was cross-cultural and on cross-cultural topics as they related to communications and psycholinguistics.

In communication, it is the strength of our external response that determines the intensity of the emotions associated with the stimulus. Our language reflects our mental processes based on our cultural context. By learning one language, we can learn another. He made a distinction between language learning and language acquisition. Two separate processes.

He also developed the semantic technique to determine the connotative context of our communication. The technique has been widely used to assess the nature of relationships and the affective meaning of people and things in our lives. Affective meaning was the focus of his studies as it related to interpersonal relationships.

He developed the GRIT strategy of reciprocity to deal with conflict through negotiation. He applied his model to the tension occurring during the nuclear arms race. Its use did help reduce the tension between the two superpowers at the time.

Additional reading: Osgood, C., Cross-Cultural Universals of Affective Meaning, University of Illinois Press, 1975.

BELONG TO A COMMUNITY

Therapy separated from life can draw many people into themselves, but they end up separating themselves from the healing communities that surround them.

Stanley Lindquist

Who said it? Dr. Stanley Lindquist (1917–2013) participated in multiple community organizations and was active in international affairs, starting with service in WWII. He had seen enough to draw the conclusion that many people are separated from a full life, such as the military, missionaries, and foreign dignitaries. He devoted his psychological knowledge to the training of relationship skills with those who are vulnerable, as they live a life that is individualistic and isolated. His active years serving "Third World People" were in the late 1900s and early 2000s.

Dr. Lindquist, while serving in the military, received life-changing injuries. He received the Purple Heart Award. He spent years in rehabilitation. Later, he returned to the university and received his Ph.D. from the University of Chicago. He taught all his academic years at Fresno State University. He formed the Link Care Counseling Center, a Christian counseling center, to serve the mental health needs of missionaries and pastors.

He held the view that when we separate ourselves from the full gamut of life of people, we end up separating ourselves also from healing communities, which we dearly need. If we separate, we also separate ourselves from any positive and beneficial input from others that could be life-supporting. Separation leads to isolation. Isolation leads to depression. Depression leads to more separation and loneliness. It is a vicious downward cycle.

As we have been doing throughout the centuries, it is easy to isolate. We tend to isolate ourselves when we are angry, anxious, upset, or depressed, as well as when we are hurt or discouraged. This is not good and is self-defeating.

As isolation leads to further depression, a vicious circle downward ensues. Lindquist advises us to get up, get out, get moving, get socializing, and get involved. Being a caring person is a lifestyle worth developing. The research supports this philosophy of life, which Dr. Lindquist advocates and teaches. It is important to learn such behavioral patterns when depressed, but it is better to learn such patterns when depression is not an immediate issue, so you have alternative problem-solving answers when depression strikes, if it does.

Additional reading: Lindquist, S., *Reach Out. . . Become an Encourager*, Creation House, 1983.

A PROFOUND OBSERVATION

Racial prejudice is inversely related to social economic status; this is how we attempt to elevate our own status.

Milton Rokeach

Who said it? Dr. Rokeach (1918–1988) was a psychiatric physician at Ypsilanti State Hospital, Ypsilanti, Michigan. Milton was a Polish-American social psychologist. He taught at several universities and was ranked as the 85th most cited psychologist of the 20th century.

In his hospital practice of psychiatry, he brought together in group therapy three male delusional and paranoid patients, each of whom believed they were Jesus Christ. He engaged them in regular group psychotherapy as a support group for each other. He confronted each with the conflicting claims of the others while encouraging them to interact personally as a support group. He attempted to manipulate and resolve aspects of their delusions by inventing messages from imaginary characters. Unfortunately, he did not provoke any lessening of the patients' delusions. He did, however, document a number of changes that occurred in their personal beliefs.

Interestingly, he was interested in and prompted to engage in this therapeutic study by an earlier study in which two females believed they were the Virgin Mary, one of whom recovered by talking to each other as roommates.

He met with the group of three men for an extensive period of time, but little good came of it, other than what we learned from him about what not to do with such patients.

He was highly criticized by many for the project on moral grounds because of the amount of dishonesty and manipulation he designed and the presumed ethical distress experienced by the three patients. It was also a concern and an area of questionable ethics for several of his colleagues.

At the end of the project, he noted that he did not affect any of the three patients. "At least we know what not to do when similar patients come into therapy," he said. He also stated at the end of the project, "It did cure me of my god-like delusions that I could manipulate them out of their beliefs." The research was published in a book by the author, which served as the basis for several musical songs, a dramatic play, and several pieces of poetry.

Further, in his ongoing research projects, one of which was on prejudice, he found "racial prejudice to be inversely related to social and economic status and thus concluded that such bias is primarily used in an attempt to elevate one's own status."

However, subsequent research refuted this claim. It does lead us to consider our own level of prejudice towards others, however. It may not be our economic status, but it is perhaps related to some experience(s) or object(s) in our past that may still operate in the present. This may be different for each person.

He held that we each must explore from which of our individual experiences in the past our personal prejudice most likely originates. This was a major component of his therapy plan for his patients.

Additional reading: Rokeach, M., *The Three Christs of Ypsilanti*, Knopf, 1974.

WHEN LIFE IS PREPLEXING

A man with a conviction is hard to change.

Leon Festinger

Who said it? Leon Festinger (1919–1989) was born in Brooklyn, New York, to a Russian immigrant family. He graduated from the City College of New York and then studied at the University of Iowa. He served as a psychologist at the Massachusetts Institute of Technology, Research Center for Group Dynamics. He later studied at the University of Minnesota. He then moved to Stanford University in 1955. He died at age 69 from liver cancer.

He taught at Stanford University, became interested in social psychology, and made the observation that people continually seek to bring order to their world, and a key part of that order is consistency. Habits and various behavioral routines are established to bring about consistency. It is associated with anxiety reduction, a sense of comfort, and inner peace. The disruption of routine brings about a sense of uneasiness. People want their lives to be consistent. Consistency gives a sense of order.

As is with daily behavior, so is with thought patterns and beliefs. We become uncomfortable and anxious if our strong opinions are met with contradictory evidence. Leon called this "cognitive dissonance." To overcome the sense of discomfort, we must make our beliefs and the behavior patterns associated with those beliefs consistent. We spend much of our time avoiding cognitive dissonance. Cognitive dissonance motivates a person to seek consistency in their life.

If there is evidence to the contrary of our strongly held beliefs, we find ourselves in an uncomfortable situation and go through a lot of unease and anxiety. This state of unrest pressures us to act in such a manner to reduce the unrest and emotional discord. He believed cognitive dissonance was the source of much of our tension and anxiety.

The state of cognitive dissonance needs to be addressed in therapy so a sense of peace can be achieved. If we accept the contradiction, this causes further inconsistency between our past and our present beliefs. So, instead, we may find ways to make the new evidence consistent with our beliefs.

Ultimately, we are driven by the desire to balance our beliefs with our behavioral patterns, so they appear to us to be consistent. If there is dissonance, there is anxiety and discomfort. We are then driven to either change our beliefs or change our behavior patterns so they become in line with each other and re-establish a sense of inner quietness. Overall, people like consistency in their lives and strive to achieve and maintain it.

Additional reading: Festinger, L., *When Prophecy Fails*, Martino Fine Press, 1956.

The Myth of Life

People often say that this or that person has not yet found himself. But the self is not something one finds; it is something one creates.

Thomas Szasz

Who said it? Dr. Szasz (1920–2012) was a well-known psychiatrist, especially known for the position he espoused regarding the non-existence of mental illness. He practiced in the last half of the 1900s. He viewed mental illness as a myth. He did not see mental illness as a separate category into which people fit. To be sure, people had problems, even serious problems, but that did not create or underscore mental illness as a person's descriptor or an identifying aspect of a person's life.

It was profound for him to espouse the idea that we don't have something called ourselves, and then lose it and then must go find it. That is nonsense, according to Dr. Szasz. The pursuit of oneself is a real and creative process. It is creative in how it is undertaken and creative in its outcome. To be sure, people can become different, see themselves differently, identify themselves differently, relate to themselves differently, and present themselves differently to others. But they still may not love themselves or see themselves as valid and valuable.

That is what we call ourselves. It deals with who I am, what I am, and what I came to become. One can find oneself, create an image of oneself, or create an identity, but still be who they are. You do not have to go anywhere; you can do it just where you are, through the process of self-reflection, therapeutic consultation, philosophical reading, spiritual undertaking, the search for meaning, and social interaction. All these steps or processes together help an individual become the full person they were created to be.

Unfortunately, for some reason and somehow, a person gets off track and does not become the person they were created to be. Hence, the search for one's personal identity and authentic lifestyle becomes a really arduous experience, and even more so for some. Unfortunately, some people spin off into never-never land in their search of themselves. Likely, they do not even know what they are seeking and would not know it if they even found it. This is a sad way to live life.

We hear it even today. Women leave the family to find themselves. Young fathers leave the family to find themselves. Husbands leave the wife and family, and wives leave the husband and family to go find themselves—whatever that is, whatever that means. It never results in finding oneself but results in a disruption of lifestyle, hurtful relationships, and pathological leftovers in the life of an entire family. The children of such parents are the ones that suffer the most, although all suffer greatly. Unfortunately for many, it is the road to destruction that leads to one's attempt to find oneself, but it does not result in any good outcome. It is like the scripture says, "There's a broad road and there's a narrow road." We stand at the fork, make that choice, and experience the results thereof.

For Szasz, it is not the finding of oneself but the development of oneself. Determine to be a fully functioning person, not one that runs away and hopes something good will come from it. Unfortunately, such pursuits are usually a false hope and an expensive exercise in futility.

The life lessons to be learned and acquired are persistent work, responsible living, and building long-term relationships. Such behavior, when learned, brings about a fully functioning and fulfilled person, not an unfulfilled hope, dream, or frenzied pursuit. One's fulfilled life is from within, not out there somewhere to be found.

He advocated against coercive treatment modalities. Modern diagnoses were seen as an outgrowth of the Inquisition.

Additional reading: Szasz, T., *The Myth of Mental Illness*, Secker and Warburg, 1961.

LIVING IN A SOCIAL WORLD

Prejudice is unloving, stupid, ignorant, and irrational.

Paul E. Meehl

Who said it? Paul Meehl (1920–2003) was born and raised in Minneapolis and taught at the University of Minnesota all of his life and career. He taught many well-known psychologists during his days of teaching. He even taught a class in philosophical psychology.

He maintained a clinical practice and utilized the theories of psychoanalysis and rational-emotive therapy.

His best-known contributions to the field of psychology were in the area of assessment. He played a key role in the development of the Minnesota Multiphasic Personality Inventory (MMPI). The MMPI has become the most widely used psychological test in the study of personality and psychopathology.

Additional reading: Meehl, P., *Thinking Clearly about Psychology: Personality and Psychopathology,* University of Minnesota Press, 1991.

YOU CANNOT REASON WITH AN UNRESONALBE PERSON

Delusional thinking separates us from others.

Paul Walzwalick

Who said it? Dr. Walzwalick (1921–2007), an Austrian psychologist, was a communication psychologist and family therapist. He practiced in the latter half of the 1900s. He is the author of twenty-two books and has taught and conducted his research at universities in Austria, Venice, Zurich, and several other countries. He is known for his "iceberg theory of communication." This viewpoint holds that only 10–20 % of all communication is factual, informative, data-based, and comprises figures. The remainder of communication is subjective, unconscious, and non-verbal. Delusional thinking easily comes from such subjective thinking and talking.

While all delusions are problematic and create life strains and stresses for individuals, it is particularly dangerous to believe that your view of reality is not only the best view but also the only correct view of reality. In other words, there is no give and take. There is no openness to learning from others. It is then easy to slip into delusional thinking. Delusional thinking promotes the idea that your own point of view is solely agreeable and worthy of consideration by all.

Such a view of reality only leads to dangerous outcomes, social rejection, isolation, and a whole series of thought patterns and conclusions shared with no one else. In fact, such thinking promotes conflict, fear, and dissonance in all relationships. Ultimately, the one with delusional thinking is rejected socially.

Further, delusional thinking isolates and separates us from others. It creates fear in others. Delusional thinking is lacking in reason and does not promote thoughtful consideration and dialogue.

It should be noted that there is a fine line between delusional thinking in an otherwise normal person and the delusional thinking and acting of a mentally ill person with psychosis. A psychotic person is considered dangerous and threatening. A person to be avoided, to be sure.

Remember the adage, "You cannot reason with an unreasonable person."

Additional reading: Watzlawick, P., *Pragmatics of Human Communication*, W.W. Norton and Company, 1967.

MEMORY CAN BE ENHANCED

We tend to remember and recall unfinished information better than information we work to complete before ending a task.

Robert Zajonc

Who said it? Dr. Zajonc (1923–2008) was born in Poland. He was captured twice during the Nazi invasion. He also escaped twice. After the second escape, he made his way to England. He later moved to the United States, where he earned his Ph.D. degree from the University of Michigan and soon established himself as an imminent social psychologist.

After retirement, he taught at Stanford and died at age 85 from cancer. He explored issues of racism, genocide, and terrorism. It appears that his individual experiences encouraged such studies. It was his hope that such research could prevent war and human suffering.

He was also known for his research findings that memory is best when material is to be learned and best remembered when it is left unfinished or incomplete. He helped create, based on this concept of unfinished tasks, what is now known as the "Zajonc Effect" in social psychology.

In 1968, he also discovered the "mere exposure effect," which is his best-known contribution to the field of social psychology. Generally speaking, previous exposure leads to more certainty and comfort, whereas novelty leads to more uncertainty, anxiety, and conflict. Novelty produces negative effects, whereas familiarity tends to produce positive effects. It was Zajonc who also established the "repeated exposure event." Repeated exposure leads to favorable identification and formidable advertising potential. This was all based on his understanding that experience accompanies, compliments, and enhances all cognition.

He also established the finding that couples grow to resemble each other in facial expression over time because they both express empathy by reflecting the same muscular facial expressions. This leads to the formation of similar facial lines. Yes, we need to smile more and develop those facial muscles so the face is more reflective of joyfulness. The more we do this together as a couple, the more both reflect a similar image or reflection. A smile begets a smile. This is also how we come to be encouraging to each other.

Additional reading: Zajonc, R., *Animal Social Psychology*, Better World Books, 1969.

DO WHAT YOU CAN DO BEST

I hate golf, so I can't retire.

Nicholas Cummings

Who said it? Dr. Cummings (1924–2020) was a tireless advocate for the development of professional psychology in America. He was instrumental in developing laws and policies for the practice and regulation of psychology. He advocated for its general acceptance within the greater medical, political, and professional communities. He, like most well-known psychologists, was endlessly engaged in the profession, both in providing therapy and in advocating for legal and constitutional advances for psychology to be generally available, like medical services, until his dying day. He was a strong advocate for the full practice of psychology and its general acceptance and availability. His contributions span the 1900s.

It is commonly thought that retirement is the onset of a second career, such as golf. Dr. Cummings, like so many others, did not know what retirement really was. Dr. Cummings did not golf or engage in the usual sporting events throughout his life. He continued to focus his efforts on psychology and its place in the world today. Retirement for the sake of golf would be like walking away from something he loved. He could not do that.

Retirement with golf is still a lifestyle for many. Many choose that path or a similar path. To Dr. Cummings, it seemed a waste of time and talent, as well as a waste of opportunity.

Astute scholars in psychology throughout history have maintained their focus on professional advancement, professional service, and professional opportunity throughout their lives. Successful and achievement-oriented people are commonly known for their tireless and endless professional activities in the professional career they are served throughout their lives. Most do not engage in "play" behavioral choices.

For those younger psychologists coming up through the ranks, it seems to be different. Many look forward to a life of "retirement." Unfortunately, the passion for psychological advancement through social action or scientific research does not appear to burn brightly in today's population of young psychologists. There are no more Nic Commings.

By looking into the lifestyle and work style of people like Nic Cummings, we have a role model of diligent and determined commitment to the field of psychology and to its advancement as a profession. Yes, to be a psychologist is important, but to bring forward the field of psychology as others have over the centuries is even more vital. What others brought to us, it is now time for us to bring an advanced field of study to the next generation.

A second lesson is the necessity of having an active and challenging task or project in which to engage if one is to retire. Golf may not fit the definition for many, as it did not for Nic. He believed that we each are to find our own creative venture and become fully engaged throughout life.

Additional reading: Cummings, N., *Psyche's Prophet*, Routledge, 2017.

A PARADOX

For the black man, there is only one destiny. And it is white.

Frantz Fanon

Who said it? Dr. Fanon (1925–1961) spoke from a world of experience in living with and relating to people of many racial differences and commonalities. He gave much thought to the issue of racism. His thinking was profound and thoughtful. He practiced psychiatry and studied colonized people in the early 1900s.

Freud and other psychiatric pioneers had an influence on Dr. Fanon. Stanford-educated. He studied the effects of racism on individuals, particularly on people of color, and the economic and psychological impact of imperialism. He spent much of his time in France. He served as the head of the psychiatric hospital in Algiers.

He authored the book, *Black Skins, White Masks*. It was one of the first attempts to understand what another race experienced in daily life and their feelings about being a member of a particular race. The 1961 book *Black Like Me* by John Howard Griffin was another similar attempt to understand the racial divide in America. The book became a movie in 1964.

For if you see yourself as black, then the only hope for a future is to be different, which is being white. If that is the case, you spend your whole life denying who you are and what you can become and seeking something that you really cannot ever become. However, if you see yourself as a man, a person, a woman, or an individual, then there is no such thing as black or white. There is nothing to pursue and nothing to avoid. There is nothing to go after, nothing to walk away from. A person lives fully to become a fulfilled person. A person without color, so to speak. A person without restrictions and without narrow boundaries. A person who can live fully, openly, and expansively and become all that he was meant to be and for which he was created.

For Fanon, we live in a very racially and genderly charged and divided world today. We have encouraged people to become something they are not and can never be. We have encouraged people to look at others and compare themselves to others rather than look within themselves. To be truly a full person, one starts by accepting oneself for who he or she is, the person he or she was created to be, and the purpose for which they were created. Our challenge is to fulfill who we are and what we are, not to dream an impossible dream or fantasy to become something we are not, never can be, and will never be.

He and his book opened for discussion the difference between ethnic and cultural differences. Essentially, a country, such as America, can be ethnically diverse but not culturally diverse. Ethnic diversity builds up a country, while cultural diversity breaks down a country.

Additional reading: Fanon, F., Black Skins; *Black Skins, White Masks*, Tantor, 1952.

GENDER IDENITY IS LEARNED

Children learn their gender (and sexual) identity through reinforcement and observational learning.

Albert Bandura

Who said it? Albert Bandura (1925–2021) was a professor at Stanford for most of the 1900s. Dr. Bandura was born in Alberta, Canada, and graduated from the University of British Columbia and the University of Iowa. He taught all his life at Stanford University. He was the recipient of many awards of distinction as a psychologist and served as president of the American Psychological Association.

He distinguished himself by researching children and how they learn within their own social context, be it the playground, preschool, home, or school. Dr. Bandura focused his research on the hypothesis that children learn aggression through observing and imitating the violent acts of peers and adults, particularly family members.

It is when a child becomes a young adult that he is able to execute an action plan so that situations in his life and in the world in which he lives can be addressed, managed, and corrected as needed.

One of the important goals of childhood is to become effective in all areas of daily living. Parents and pre-school teachers are the primary teachers of self-management and self-control. Only then is one ready to face the daily experiences of living a stress-filled and complicated life.

Dr. Bandura brings to us the crucial point that it is our responsibility to learn how to organize our lives and surroundings first and foremost. This starts at home by learning how to organize a room, school desk, homework, or one's chores so that productivity results. It is then that a child becomes a young adult and can execute an action plan so that situations in his life and in the world in which he lives can be addressed, managed, and corrected as needed.

He did recognize that Skinner's views were important and that positive reinforcement is a strong factor in influencing the direction of our behavior. He also recognized that Freud had a valid point in that people assimilate the characteristics of others into their own personalities.

The most famous work by Bandura was his research with Bobo Dolls in 1977, which led him to develop his own treatise on social learning theory.

The research of Bandura formed the observation of gender and sexual identity He believed that because their parents, other significant adults, and peers treat them differently and uniquely, children frequently display differences in their behavior. Adults tailor their behavior toward children from birth to match their own gender role expectations. This encourages children to behave according to what is considered a gender norm.

Further, whatever behavior is reinforced is strengthened and becomes a pattern of behavior, as was well established by B.F. Skinner. The reinforcement to which children are exposed subtly encourages them to behave in a manner that is sex-appropriate. Sex-appropriate behavior is learned from early childhood. For Bandura, it was the discovery of how kids become sexual and gender balanced and coordinated that was the key task of the parents.

Additional reading: Bandura., A., *Social Foundations of Thought and Action: A Social Cognitive Theory*, Pearson, 1986.

HAPPINESS IS SELF-DETERMINED

For happy people, time is filled and planned. For unhappy people, time is unfilled, open, and uncommitted. We postpone things and are inefficient.

Michael Argyle

Who said it? Dr. Argyle (1925–2002) was a British psychologist focusing his research efforts on effective and ineffective communication styles. He was one of the best-known British psychologists of the 19th century. He discovered that the non-verbal signals we give out are often more important and powerful than our verbal communication when conveying feelings and attitudes.

Happiness is well-identified. It results from who we are and how we live. It does not determine how to live. If our lives are organized, planned, and put into perspective each day, happiness is a resulting experience for that day, and each day we live a life that is planned and organized.

Happiness has been a concept throughout history that has been important to people. It is usually referred to because of how we live. It is not thought to be the basis for our lifestyle or choices in life. So, if we want to be happy people, start living a life that is organized, planned, systematized, routine, managed, and thought out. Happiness results accordingly. This is a situation in which the cart and the horse must be in the right order and have the right relationship with each other. Indeed, the horse before the cart.

He also held the view that the mind, which is still the whole universe, surrenders. Learning how to quiet a busy mind is the key to happiness and health.

Additional reading: Argyle, M., *The Psychology of Happiness*, Routledge, 1987.

Social Influence

If you put good apples in a bad situation, you'll get bad apples.

Philip G. Zimbardo

Who said it? Philip G. Zimbardo (1933–), a professor of psychology at Stanford, has distinguished himself not only as a professor but also as a cognitive behavioral therapist to students on campus and to young people in his community. He is aware of the statement he popularized, "People are like apples." We are influenced by the environment, by those with whom we have limited contact, and especially by those with whom we spend a lot of time.

The message for all of us is to gain an understanding of how we are influenced by others around us and how we influence those with whom we spend time. Apples become bad apples in the same way that bad people beget bad people. It is vitally important that our relationships are pure, genuine, and absent or void of various kinds of "bad influence."

He showed how good people turn evil and become abusive under positions of power and control. This was shown in his famous experiments with prison guards.

Dr. Zimbardo puts his finger on the pulse. In today's world, especially in our young population, we see the ground swell of influence that permeates a school, a playground, a community, and even a nation. Bad apple exposes others to the thought processes and interpersonal components that generate negativity, violence, destruction, and hurt upon others, who in turn perpetrate those same kinds of life experiences upon others. The violent masses that were responsible for the burning of many cities in our country—Minneapolis, Seattle, and Portland, to name a few—came about through the process of a bad apple imposing itself upon other apples and turning them into bad apples, who in turn generated bad apples among others, and so on. It's a process.

It's an insidious and nefarious process of personal and interpersonal destruction that openly leads to the destruction of one's community, society, and country.

Additional reading: Zimbardo, P., *The Time Paradox*, Atria, 2008.

MARRIAGES THAT STICK

Don't marry the person you think you can live with;
marry the person you cannot live without.

James Dobson

Who said it? Dr. Dobson (1936–2018) is well-known for his psychological insights and leadership for parents in raising children and for young marriages launching off into their new world together. Dr. Dobson played a major role in shaping political thought and action during the Ronald Reagan presidential years on relevant topics related to psychology and the family.

He served on President Reagan's Task Force on Pornography. One major assignment was to serve on the commission to study the effects of pornography on the family. His active years of family life influence were in the latter part of the 1900s and early 2000s. He formed the well-known organizations Focus on the Family and the Family Research Council. He is responsible for the significant increase in people coming to therapy and benefiting from it. He made therapy and counseling acceptable to the general population.

Dr. Dobson well understands marriage. We often hear that young couples seek ways to see if they can live together. Many of them justify pre-marital cohabitation based on whether two lives can be better meshed by living together in pre-marital cohabitation.

However, Dodson disagrees and dispels that idea. The research data indicates that divorce is the most common among those who cohabit before marriage. This finding is still the prevailing outcome of co-habitation. Further, he held that research supported the view that cohabiting before marriage is not healthy and does not serve to answer the ultimate question of not being able to live without the other person. The divorce rate among marriages after cohabituating is unusually high.

The individuals must decide whether their perceptive mate is something they cannot live without. That is profound. That implies two dynamics. First, somebody who needs what you have to offer; and second, someone who has what you need to receive in a relationship. Thus, making a relationship unique, spiritual, honorable, and fulfilling for both.

It is true, as marriage has been part of life forever and forever will be. Marriages are not to be a relationship that you enter and then disregard at some point.

Marriage relationships are meant to be fulfilling throughout a lifetime. That can only happen when a couple makes the decision that they cannot live without each other. They need each other, draw strength from each other, and contribute strength to each other.

Additional reading: Dobson, J., *Bringing Up Boys*, Tyndale House, 2021.

OUR VALUES ARE LEARNED

Until you value yourself, you won't value your time. Until you value your time, you will not do anything with it.

M. Scott Peck

Who said it? Dr. Peck (1936–2005) was a well-versed spokesperson for positive psychology. His sudden death deprived all of us of his ongoing wisdom, advice, and support. This phrase gives a sense of his thinking and his sensitivity for people. He ended his practice at the time of his death. He died a premature death just as his psychiatric career was beginning to flourish. He had just authored the best-selling book, *A Road Less Traveled*. In the book, he proposes that much of life is a choice, such as marriage. A couple comes to a point in their relationship where they choose to marry and live together, as they cannot live without each other. He was an approachable man and impacted many in his short years of clinical practice, teaching, and writing.

Dr. Peck realized life is difficult. That realization is the beginning point of living life fully and honestly. We then come to understand life and accept it for what it is. Life then becomes less difficult as we can step out of our rut and search for the true answers to life's questions. Ultimately, life is not a problem or a bunch of problems to be solved, but a mystery to be lived.

Dr. Peck considered self-discipline essential for emotional, spiritual, and psychological health. It is the means for spiritual evolution. He also emphasized accepting responsibility and the need to be able to delay gratification as essential to full health in all areas of life.

His book addresses issues for parents, newlyweds, seekers of spirituality, and all those seeking the fullness of life.

To be sure, we are all similar but different. Similarities are to be shared, appreciated, and utilized so that we together can accomplish and achieve. There is always greater achievement when two or more people work together than when a task is undertaken alone.

Furthermore, Dr. Peck clearly spoke to the idea of differences and put them into perspective. Differences are to be celebrated. To be sure, we are different in color, race, and in many subtle ways. Differences are not to be feared or exploited but should be enjoyed as a source of enrichment for all. He put it this way: "We are similar, yet different. Fear our similarities; celebrate our differences."

Additional reading: Peck, M.S., *A Road Less Traveled*, Touchstone, 1978.

THE TRUE MARRIAGE

Marriages sizzle when the needs of both spouses are satisfied.

Willard F. Harley, Jr.

Who said this? Dr. Harley (1941–) was a teacher, writer, counselor, and the founder of a series of marriage counseling centers throughout Minnesota. He was masterful at helping couples identify their respective needs and then help them live in such a way that the needs of each were fulfilled. The ten most vital needs of men and women were identified and expounded upon. When needs are mutually met, marriages are safe and free of extramarital affairs and other destructive events.

He is best known for his four major accomplishments. He is the author of an internationally best-selling book, *His Needs, Her Needs: Building an Affair-proof Marriage*. It has sold over four million copies and been translated into over twenty-two foreign languages. Secondly, Dr. Harley is well-known as an effective teacher of psychology, both at the undergraduate and graduate levels. Thirdly, he was an effective marriage counselor and designed his own approach to marital counseling. Fourthly, he developed a series of twenty-two mental health clinics throughout the state of Minnesota. The clinics became the exclusive providers of mental health and chemical dependency services throughout Minnesota. He has written over nineteen books. He speaks and leads seminars throughout the United States and Canada. He provides seminars under the title *How to Fall in Love and Stay in Love*.

For Dr. Harley, romantic love is not superficial, trivial, or fleeting. It is purposeful. It is need-meeting-focused. The focus is on each other and the meeting of each other's needs. In a relationship, the other person is foremost. Needs are to be expressed in the context of the relationship. Only then will a marriage flourish and be free of self-destructive conflict-behavior patterns. He goes on to assure us that a marriage can be more than a dream; it can be one's reality.

Marriages with blended families tend to be very unsuccessful, which is one of the greatest predictors of divorce. It is common for each spouse to put their own children's interests first.

Mutual satisfaction is the issue to be addressed in any marriage counseling program. Until a couple comes to recognize and appreciate the needs of each other, problems will be on their horizon, to be sure. Dr. Harley devotes his program in marriage counseling to teaching couples how to communicate their needs and how to coordinate the behaviors necessary to meet their respective needs.

The average American couple needs more of Dr. Harley and his like. Marriages are in trouble all over the country. Family life is at an all-time low. Dr. Harley is needed. He held the view that the beginning point of any marriage is to recognize the needs of each other. That is where a marriage must begin. He goes on to state that marriages sizzle when the needs of both spouses are satisfied.

Additional reading: Harley, W., *His Needs, Her Needs: Making Romantic Love Last*, Revell, 1986.

LIFE EXPERIENCES SHAPE OUR LIVES

Trauma is a fact of life. It does not, however, have to be a life sentence.

Peter A. Levine

Who said it? Dr. Levine (1942–) holds a doctorate in psychology and medical biophysics. He developed the somatic experiencing and body awareness approaches to the understanding and treatment of trauma. He focuses with keen interest on the natural pathways of healing. He bases his thinking on his own traumatizing experiences as a child. He says his research was really "me-search."

We all face experiences in life that have traumatizing effects. They are often long-lasting, if not for life. Such experiences change us. Some of us survive, and some don't. Some grow stronger, and some grow weaker. Trauma is certainly life-changing. Learning to live with trauma and even living above it is an essential task for everyone who has been exposed to some type of trauma experience at some point in their life. Lavine's awareness of the trauma experience and its profound impact on a person came from a dream. It was a bottom-up process of healing. Dr. Levine taught it to all who would listen, especially young therapists and healers of all types.

As trauma is more recognized and common, we do need to learn how to process it in a healthy manner. Lavine does this for us. Confront the trauma experience and find out how to become a better and stronger person because of it. Heal and become a better person over time. Process the trauma with a trained psychologist. Become a healer of your own trauma. It need not last a lifetime.

He believed it was important to deal with one's chronic fear as part of a recovery treatment program. It does not happen without the guidance of a trained psychologist.

His research interests over the years have focused on brain injury, strokes, brain plasticity, brain trauma, and their recovery.

Additional reading: Levine, P., *Walking the Tiger*, Tantor Press, 1997.

INTELLEGENCE IS ACQUIRED

A person is not born with all the intelligence they will ever have.

Howard Earl Gardner

Who said it? Dr. Gardner (1943–) was a cognitive-developmental psychologist. Harvard trained. He was a prolific researcher and writer. He authored hundreds of papers and books. He was also a screenwriter, an actor, and a professor. It was said of him, "What does he not do?"

He conceptualized a theory of eight types or multiple intelligences. Here they are:

- Logical-Mathematical
- Linguistic
- Naturalist
- Musical
- Spatial
- Bodily Kinesthetic
- Interpersonal
- Intrapersonal

It is important to note that others more recently have proposed similar types of distinctions when describing the types and styles of brilliance of a person. A person is not born with all the intelligence they will ever have. A novel idea in his day.

There are several schools, colleges, and elementary schools globally devoted to the study of and the implementation of multiple intelligences and cognitive development.

He also focused much of his time on understanding aphasia. Such individuals are known for their speech that is nonsensical and devoid of adjectives. Speech is often mangled. He has helped us understand aphasia and how to help those with it function better.

Additional reading: Gardner, H.E., *Frames of Mind: The Theory of Multiple Intelligence*, Abe Books, 1983.

THE TRUISM OF SOCIAL INFLUENCE

We are all subject to erroneous information and act on it as if it were true.

Elizabeth Loftus

Who said it? Dr. Loftus (1944–) is one of America's leading experts on memory and factors that influence memory accuracy. Memory can be changed by things we are told, facts, ideas, suggestions, and post-event information to which we are exposed. Her work is often quoted in legal court cases on eyewitness events. She has been called an expert witness in many famous court cases. She has been recognized for her sound science and evidence on matters of public interest. Memories are not as reliable as we think they are. Much of our memory function is based on false memories.

Dr. Loftus was educated at Stanford University and spent much of her career at the University of Washington.

Her research led her to study the issue of "false memories." Many kids were led to believe they were molested as children but were actually not. This led to the repressed memory wars in the 1980s. Many professionals were sued over these issues, which became more of an emotional issue than a scientific one.

She was awarded the John Maddox Award for standing up for the science of psychology in the face of opposition.

Additional reading: Loftus, Elizebeth, *Witness for the Defense*, St. Martin's Griffen, 1991.

ACHIEVEMENT

Achievement depends on our self-image.
Becoming is better than being.

Carol S. Dweck

Who said it? Dr. Dweck (1946–) is a professor of psychology at Stanford University and focuses her research attention on how our expectations motivate us for successful living. Her primary studies span the years 1972 to the present.

Dr. Dweck espouses the idea that we are always in a state of becoming. We are becoming better. We are becoming smarter. We are becoming more worldly-wise and goal-oriented. For her, a meaningful life requires certain critical values. Such values are to be learned at home and in school. They are to be taught by parents and teachers in coordination with each other.

In contrast, a person is stuck in a non-growth pattern when they are satisfied with being what they are and have achieved. How we structure our expectations and image of ourselves currently and futuristically largely determines how we behave and what we achieve, or lack thereof.

The teaching of values is critical for parents to do at home. Parents need to accept their role as teachers of their children, not just caretakers. In a way, parents "grow" their children to become fully developed and mature young adults. Parents as well as teachers do serve in the role of "gardeners" and proceed to raise children into mature adults. It has been said, "Parents are a child's first teacher." Parents need to feel honored to be so identified and take their responsibility seriously.

Additional reading: Dweck, Carol, *Mindset: The New Psychology of Success*, Abe Books, 2006.

LOVE COMES IN MANY FORMS

Reciprocity is the highest form of love. And love has everything to do with healing.

Michele DeKleverns Ritterman

Who said it? Dr. DeKleverns Ritterman (1946–) was one of the foremost students of the psychoanalyst Milton Erickson. She was noted for her expertise regarding survivors of political torture and their families. She specialized in family therapy and hypnotherapy, collaborating in therapy with survivors of trauma and torture.

According to Dr. Ritterman, love is a maturing process. It grows with the maturation of a relationship. A relationship grows on reciprocity. It is giving, giving, and giving as one has been given to, even more so. It is a reciprocal relationship of giving, sharing, commonality, interests, support, encouragement, and affirmation. Unless one is in a reciprocal relationship, that relationship is not a loving one. It is more than taking from each other and keeping a balance sheet. All reciprocal relationships start with sharing mutuality and mutually giving to each other. There is no score-keeping. It is just a matter of mutual sharing, mutually giving, mutually helping, mutual benefit, and companionship.

Further, she states that the reciprocal relationship in a marriage is an ever-present aspect of being healthy, loving, growing, maturing, and enhancing the relationship. Relationships do not grow unless there is reciprocal interaction, reciprocal caring, and reciprocal sharing. If one wonders about one's own marriage and loving relationships, one needs to look no further than the degree to which reciprocity is systematically present in those relationships.

The Biblical teaching of "doing unto others as you would have them do unto you" is essential to the establishment of positive behavior patterns. One could do no better than to build strong relationships with others. To be sure, not only will the marriage thrive, but it will also have a positive influence on others, such as friends, neighbors, and business associates. Positive relationships open doors of opportunity and personal growth for all involved.

Symptoms are identified as a trance state. Therapy is then the production of counter-inductions and hypnotic sequences that impact the symptom trance, as Milton Erickson would describe it. Dr. Rittterman blended hypnosis and family therapy together. She was especially sensitive to and opposed to socially abusive governments. She is described as a unique woman and therapist.

Additional reading: Ritterman, M., *The Tao of a Woman*, Jossey Bass, 2000.

THOUGHT PATTERNS SEEKS LIMITS

It is not primarily our physical selves that limit us, but rather our mindset about our physical limits.

Ellan J. Langer

Who said it? Dr. Langer (1947–) is a Harvard University professor whose research focuses on mindfulness, which has a strong influence on a range of fields of study, from behavioral science to economics and beyond. She was the first woman to be tenured in psychology at Harvard.

Mindfulness, one of her fields of study, has been shown to reduce stress, increase charisma and self-esteem, and improve work performance, such as in the fields of sales and sports. She developed a 21-item scale to measure individual differences regarding the trait of mindfulness from a socio-cognitive point of view. The three components of mindfulness are novelty seeking, creativity and flexibility, and engagement. Essentially, it is mind-openness. Due to her early studies on mindfulness, she became known as the "Mother of Mindfulness."

To be sure, we are limited by our own physical strength, agility, and coordination abilities. However, the primary factor that either minimizes our disability or maximizes our attitude about it is different for each person. If our physical limitations create a sense of anger, resentment, and bitterness, we will never overcome or go beyond our limitations. However, if we have an attitude of hope, faith, and possibility, then our physical limitations are minimal, and we function at least at a level of practical functionality. Remember, it is not what happened to us, but how we react to it. It is how we view it.

Physical limitations have always been with us; however, we have now learned that our physical limitations can be minimized or maximized by our attitudes. Hence, it is more of an issue of attitude than of physical or mental limitations. It is more our reaction and attitude than an event, state of mind, or our body itself. Had a strong influence on positive psychology as a growing area of study.

Langer has also devoted much of her research time to the study of aging globally. Flexibility in the aging process has been a critical component of her studies.

Her studies on "counterclockwise" were famous and served as the basis of reminiscence therapy.

To be sure, she is a very accomplished psychologist.

Additional reading: Langer, E., *Counterclockwise*, Oxford University Press, 2009.

CREATIVITY

Creativity involves breaking out of established patterns in order to look at things in a different way.

Edward de Bono

Who said this? Creativity, according to Dr. de Bono (1933–), is considered important to us. Creativity is a critical and important trait for us to develop. It is one of the traits associated with effective, independent living. His studies in thinking encouraged him to advocate for the teaching of thinking skills and strategies in schools at all levels.

Creativity became a subject of considerable study in the 1960s. Much of it was aimed at identifying children and adults who are creative and determining how they function differently from non-creative people. Also, how they need to be taught differently in the classroom was also a subject of much interest to Drs. De Bono, Grotberg, Pielstik, and others.

Whenever a child or adult breaks out of established patterns of behavior, they give indications of creativity. It is through creativity that the world opens, and we are able to see things that otherwise we would not see. Further, we understand things that we otherwise would not understand, and we contribute to society in ways in which we would not contribute otherwise.

Breaking out of established patterns of behavior, established patterns of thinking, and established patterns of social relationships with others is fresh, exciting, and exhilarating. Indeed, creativity needs to be appreciated, encouraged, and taught.

Additional reading: de Bono, E., *Six Thinking Hats*, Little Brown and Company, 1985.

INTERPERSONAL INFLUENCE

If you put good apples in a bad situation, you'll get bad apples.

Philip G. Zimbardo

Who is it? Dr. Zimbardo (1933–) is a professor of psychology at Stanford University. He focuses his research efforts on the social behavior of individuals. He is noted for his research on shyness and how to help shy individuals overcome this particular disorder. He had many research interests, based on the research paradigm of the prisoner's dilemma. This research demonstrated the power of social situations to influence the behavioral choices of people. Unfortunately, it is not always for the best.

When speaking about good and bad apples, he draws from his research in psychology, which clearly indicates that you become like and take on the likeness of those with whom you associate. This is particularly true with those with whom you have close associations.

While a psychologist cannot tell people what to do, this quote is certainly applicable and predictive. It indicates what will happen to an individual if they associate with others who are considered "bad apples." The role of the psychologist or therapist is to help guide people away from associations and relationships that are potentially and eventually destructive. It was important to him that people learn to be assertive and enter into healthy relationships.

In contrast, psychologists want people to associate with "good apples" and thereby benefit from their influence. It is from a batch of "good apples" that healthy people thrive. However, his research established that we are not always good people. There is an evil part to all of us, unfortunately.

Additional reading: Zimbardo, P., *The Lucifer Effect*, Random House, 2007.

THE REQUIREMENTS OF SELF-IMPROVEMENT

The ideal patient is willing to engage in self-reflection, explore the deeper existential issues related to his predicament, and discover the pathways to actualizing his or her potential and dream.

Paul Wong

Who said this? Dr. Wong (1937–2018) is a Canadian-based psychologist who has devoted his professional career to the understanding and teaching of meaning and its role in our overall health and personal happiness. The meaning of faith is one of the primary foci of his research.

He is of the opinion that we need to experience personal growth and learn how to flourish while simultaneously reducing the dark side of life associated with depression, anxiety, and anger. Only then can personal self-actualization come about, according to Dr. Wong.

The most effective treatment is deficiency-focused and personal strength-based. Patients must face and repair the worst aspects of their lives while simultaneously bringing out their best. A therapist must be attuned spiritually and culturally to the patient for the best results to be achieved. All therapy must be tailor-made to the unique needs and concerns of the patient. The patient-doctor compatibility factor is one of the guiding principles for therapy to be purpose-driven and effective overall. Wong goes on to state that an ideal patient has an expressed need to change his life. This is what serves as the foundational stone for therapy and the basis for enhanced meaning in life.

In his writings, he has addressed the issues of meaning, culturalism, suffering, stress and coping, death, and spirituality.

He produces a pod cast for one minute, "Nuggets of Wisdom." He continues to be an active author. His most recent book, entitled *A Second-Wave Positive Psychology in Counseling Psychology,* was published in 2023.

Additional reading: Wong, P., *The Human Quest for Meaning*, Routledge, 1998.

BE AWARE OF YOUR IMPACT ON OTHERS

You generally get back what you send out. If you are kind to others, they will tend to be kind to you. If you are hostile, you can expect to find that other people are hostile too. If you are unhappy with how people treat you, think about your persona.

C. Eugene Walker

Who said it? Dr. Walker (1939–) focused most of his career on child medical psychology. While teaching at Baylor University and the University of Oklahoma Medical School, he distinguished himself by addressing various medical problems of children as a psychologist while also teaching the psychological components of children's medical disorders to psychological and medical students. His primary practice was conducted in the latter part of the 1900s and early 2000s. It was important to him that medical residents learned to consider the psychological components of illnesses and disorders. This emphasis contributed to the depth of training for physicians.

For example, Dr. Walker taught physicians in training to understand that giving and receiving are reciprocally related. How we project ourselves onto our patients and within all our relationships to a greater extent determines how we are responded to and treated by others. If a physician changes how he or she responds and reacts to others, then others will change accordingly in response. This is how all relationships, especially doctor-patient relationships, flourish, thrive, or become distressed and dysfunctional.

As this has been true throughout history, it is also true today and will be in the future. We are social beings, and particularly reactive social beings. Few of us live above the day-to-day fray of complex human relationships. We are well advised to be thoughtful, wise, and careful in our social relationships. We are also advised to be responsive and not reactive in our dealings with our patients, staff, and others. This results in a good life for all. The best doctor-patient relationship is based on trust and likeability for each other. That is essential for the good outcome of any medical or therapeutic procedure.

Additional reading: Walker, C. and Roberts, M., *Handbook of Clinical Child Psychology*, Wiley Publisher, 2001.

WELL-BEING IS A COMPLEX STATE

Well-being cannot just exist in your own head. Well-being is a combination of feeling good as well as actually having meaning, good relationships, and accomplishments.

Martin Seligman

Who said it? Martin Seligman (1942–) was the spokesperson for and formulator of positive psychology. His point was to get away from the negativism of mental illness and mental health and look at behavior and the lives of people from a more positive point of view. He charted a whole new course in psychology, emphasizing hope, healthy relationships, and thinking futuristically. He actively taught at the University of Pennsylvania and practiced during the mid-1900s.

Dr. Seligman put his finger on the pulse of having hope and having a happy future. It is not just a matter of feeling good. That is not good enough. It is having meaning, purpose, and a sense of value that comes from and is intermingled with positive and healthy relationships. A series of accomplishments and the hope of future accomplishments were considered of significant importance for healthy living. Well-being is a result of what we do and how we live. Well-being is the result of our efforts, lifestyle, and relationships that we enjoy and engage in regularly. Positive psychology refocused our attention on resilience, learned helplessness, depression prevention, and optimism.

For example, happiness, an area of much study, can be cultivated if we live a pleasant life, a good life, and a meaningful life. Further, gratitude, one's physical health, and mindfulness are also contributing factors for happiness to prevail. However, the number one rule for happiness is to have a strong social network.

Additional reading: Seligman, M., *Flourish*, Atria, 2012.

OUR HUMAN POTENTIAL

Many people think that discipline is the essence of parenting. But that is not parenting. Parenting is not telling your child what to do when she or he misbehaves. Parenting is providing the conditions under which a child can realize his or her full human potential.

Gordon Neufeld

Who said it? Dr. Neufeld (1946–) is a Canadian-based psychologist specializing in family relationships, parenting, and child development. He focuses his teaching, research, and writing on helping parents become less controlling of their children while still providing the necessary protection, support, and care every child needs. The overriding goal is to assist a child in their development as human beings and live out their full potential.

Unfortunately, many parents terminate their parenting responsibilities early, even too early in the life of a child. They let their children become independent long before they were ready for the steps of independence and self-management. Children who are prematurely released from parental care and guidance have a much tougher time realizing their human potential and often become the victims of neglect and loneliness. Parents are not to control their children but to gradually release them into a world of independence with the necessary and ongoing support, basic knowledge, self-help skills, and good problem-solving and decision-making skills. Parents have alternative courses of action to take. But it is vital to keep control in the hands of the parents and in the home.

Additional reading: Neufeld, G., *Hold on to your kids: Why Parents Need to Matter More than Peers*, Aona Books, 2013.

KINDNESS IS ACQUIRED

Be kind to others. The first person to experience your kindness is yourself.

Michael S. Kesselman

Who said it? Dr. Kesselman (1946–) practiced clinical psychology throughout the latter part of the 1900's and the early 2000's. He has devoted his practice to those workers who have been injured in their line of work and during work hours. He is personally known by his patients for his gentleness and kindness. He is known likewise among his colleagues and friends. He urges his patients to show kindness despite their injuries and life circumstances. His life is a model for others to exhibit kindness in their sphere of influence.

Dr. Kesselman speaks of kindness as a personal quality so much needed in the world today. It is a quality that is present in high-functioning relationships. Kindness is a learned behavior from childhood. Parents are the primary teachers of this important trait.

To be sure, kindness starts in the home and within the parent-child relationship and interactional patterns. Being kind to oneself starts in the home and, over time, grows, matures, and expands to others and the general community.

To express kindness towards others and to live a life based on kindness in all interpersonal relationships is a most worthy goal for all of us. Every parent needs to make it the basic skill taught in the home through example and instructional teaching.

Psychological studies underscore the importance of kindness in all our relationships and in every area of life. Kindness is a primary antidote to depression, for example. It also facilitates people connecting with each other, another way to combat depression and avoid loneliness.

The origins and importance of kindness are underscored in the Biblical script, in which we are admonished to be "kind one to another." We can do no better. Kindness was also the basic value inherent within the hospital treatment system and patient management of the psychiatric asylums of the 1800s. It has been a basic value of all well-functioning societies throughout history. It has stood the test of time in human relationships at all levels.

Note: Not being a wordsmith, Dr. Kesselman focused his professional time on rendering services for injured workers and providing them with kindness, a much-needed quality response from his patients.

PLAY BEGETS SOCIAL DEVELOPMENT

Free play is an important part of child development.
It is where they learn things like courage, creativity, and social skills.

Peter Gray

Who said it? Dr. Gray (1946–) is a Boston University professor specializing in educational problems in our local schools. Our educational system is stuck and needs help to get unstuck. Dr. Gray is giving us guidance in dealing with classroom behavior and problems. He has a special interest in the relationship between educational success and play.

It is important to note that child development takes place in relation to the amount of play in which a child engages. Parents must encourage and arrange for daily free play time. As a result, creativity is developed along with independence and socialization skills. Parents are well advised to schedule and plan for free play to take place at home. Parents need to be actively connected with their children through play. Play is too important to allow it to be avoided or neglected. Dr. Gray as well as Dr. Piaget agree that play is the work of children.

Parents also need to deal with the issues of cell phones, social media, and video viewing. Specify times to have non-video free time and when and where to have video game time, for example.

Parents might be well advised to engage in free play themselves and set an example for their children. Parents can help teach free play by playing with their children more often. In so doing, create games and toys to be used in playing some homemade games. Like a lot of things with children, it starts in the home and with the parents. He did not encourage parents to be helicopter parents.

Additional reading: Gray, P., *Free to Learn*, Basic Books, 2015.

The WORLD OF THE UNKNOWN

You will never know if you do not try.

Deborah Ohanesian

Who said it? Dr. Ohanesian (1946–) has offered this piece of advice to overcome fear to her therapy patients for years. Many get stuck in their fear and do not even try to capitalize on the opportunities before them. She admits she is the product of this self-defeating fear. Only when she ventured beyond her comfort zone did she realize she could do more and achieve more than she believed. Once she addressed the fear head-on, she soon overcame the fear and lived with much more confidence thereafter. She has found that others often had more faith in her than she had in herself. This self-defeating thinking is self-destructive and achievement-contradictory.

Fear stops us. Fear immobilizes us. Fear limits our range of experience, creativity, and achievements. Sometimes it takes another person in our lives to come along with us and nudge us out of our fear-based comfort zone. Only then do we experience a higher level of living, happiness, and achievement. Freedom, according to Dr. Ohanesian, is living beyond our fears.

Sometimes we are the ones who nudge another person to go forth and succeed in some life-time desire, opportunity, or venture. Those who nudge others to go beyond their comfort zone or skill level are called "agents of change." The call is for us as therapists to live a life as change agents for others in our world of influence. We are the ones to lead our patients into a life of freedom.

To be sure, anyone who nudges another person benefits as well. The professional who nudges another, something that is done all day long, acts out of love and for the best interest of the patient. Both benefits. We as therapists are not to encourage behaviors that are elevated risk or life-changing without all the proper safeguards for the patient and with the appropriate informed consent.

Note: Instead of authoring a book or articles, Dr. Ohanesian has focused her attention on her patients, especially those processing through the immigration system legally.

HISTORICAL CONTRIBUTIONS IN PSYCHOLOGY

1950 - 2000

THE ESSENCE OF SCIENCE

The field of psychology advances based on the empirical data from our research.

Marvin McDonald

Who said it? Dr. McDonald (1952–) is a Canadian-based psychologist who has devoted his career to the study of and teaching of psychology and faith and how they relate. How psychology and faith are integrated is his prime interest. The purpose of his teaching on the faculty of Trinity Western University is to focus on the training of faith-based psychologists who will serve in mental health counseling centers throughout Canada. His research passion has focused on the positive psychology of meaning and spirituality. His other areas of research are family psychology and cultural identity development. He takes considerable pride in teaching students to integrate their studies of psychology and faith.

Scientifically based therapy is how patients progress in resolving their personal problems and stresses. In contrast, "pop-psychology" is how most untrained or limited therapists approach a person's problem. It is like giving common-sense advice while relying on slogans and metaphors. People take their therapy seriously and are desperate for a positive outcome. Every therapist, he thought, must spend time reading research on faith and advanced studies in the treatment of all dysfunctions brought to their attention for professional help.

Holding to the position that science advances on the findings of the research it conducts, he takes seriously the training of young psychologists in the scientific methods of research. He also focuses on multi-cultural counseling and collaborative assessment. Knowing the research findings and using them in the psychological services provided is vital to him. For example, more women than men seek the help of a counselor. Men have higher rates of substance abuse and addiction.

For McDonald, research findings provided the guidance every therapist needs in addressing the problems presented by patients every day. Without such guidance, a therapist can revert to "junk science" and just become another voice of opinion.

Additional reading: McDonald, M., *Mind and Brain, Science and Religion: Belief and Neuroscience,* University Press of America., 1996.

OUR NEW BEGINNING

Learning begins literally from the time babies are born, and there's even some evidence that there is learning inside the womb.

Allison Gopnik

Who said it? Dr. Gopnik (1955–) is a professor of psychology at the University of California, Berkeley. Dr. Gopnik emphasizes the importance of early learning and underscores the role of parents in providing the foundational stones of learning for a child. She engages in research to explore how young children come to know about the world around them. Parenting style is a critical area of study for her. How do kids develop under different parenting styles?

The quotation is an especially critical issue for parental guidance in rearing children. To be sure, children learn from birth onward. Hence, parents are the first teachers' children ever have. One would even say that parents are the first and most important teachers a child ever has. Children continue to learn throughout life and build on the foundational stones of their early childhood education in the home.

Every child starts with homeschooling. Parents need to give serious thought to what they teach and how they instruct their children during the formative years of life. The sound and tone of the voice are extremely critical. The behavioral patterns portrayed by the parents in front of their children are also important and have a lasting effect. Children learn from observation just as well as from instruction.

When it comes to pre-birth learning, the evidence seems to suggest that children learn by association. They associate sound with emotional arousal. For example, loud and frightening sounds create emotional arousal in the fetus, which can be well-established and then continue throughout childhood and adulthood. This may account for the reason some people are chronically anxious, fearful, and unforthcoming throughout life. The lifestyle of a pregnant mother and those in her life provide the emotional foundation through the conditioning and learning processes of children. All pre-birth experiences are critical to how a person approaches life throughout life.

Additional reading: Gopnik, A., *The Gardiner and the Carpenter,* Farrar, Straus, and Gioux, 2016.

TEACHING LIFE TO KIDS

Getting alone with family, friends, and others requires the character trait of respect.

Don Mac Mannis

Who said this? Dr. Mac Mannis, a.k.a. Dr. Mac (1959–), referred to as "Dr. Mac," is a child psychologist who teaches children important truths about life's songs in therapy. He is a "singing psychologist." He has produced many songs and rhymes, which he uses in his therapy with children. He is active in teaching and training young, up-and-coming therapists as interns.

Respect is one of the basic attitudes and values for children to learn in their socialization process. When we respect others, we create an atmosphere of kindness and pleasantness. In such relationships, children thrive socially, emotionally, and intellectually. Respect is also a basic component of positive psychology, which promotes character development and social grace in daily life. Imagine being a child in therapy with Dr. Mac Mannis and singing a song and talking about kindness.

Throughout history, singing has always been part of children's upbringing. Songs and choruses always had a value or life skill to teach. This was most often taught to children in summer camps, Sunday school, boys and girls clubs, and so on. Dr. Mac Mannis does it in his office during therapy hours with his young clients.

He has organized a six-week school series of lessons using songs to teach the basics of social values and life skills to young children. Positive results have been tracked when these lessons are utilized.

Parents are encouraged to arrange for poetry and singing time with their children. After a meal is an enjoyable time for this type of activity.

His therapy approach is based on an emphasis on being supportive, integrative, community-oriented, and research-based.

Additional reading: Mannis, D., *How's Your Family Really Doing? 10 Keys to a Happy, Loving Family*, CreateSpace, 2011.

THE NATURAL DESTRESSOR

The body calms down after 90 seconds.

Jill Bolte-Taylor

Who said it? Dr. Bolte-Tylor (1959–2006) formulated the 90-second rule of stress management in 2006. Her research on stress led to the conclusion that stress can be managed and that it has a time factor regarding its intensity and impact. Stress is related to adrenaline production. The level of adrenaline produced during stress gradually reduces over time and comes down to a manageable level. That period is 90 seconds. She practices as a neuroscientist. She is well known for her analysis of her own stroke and her recovery. She writes and speaks more similarly to that of a psychologist than a neurologist.

When a person can manage stress, productive and functional behavior results. Panic reaction patterns result from the belief that the initial flow of adrenalin will be overwhelming, uncontrollable, and destructive. Thankfully, this is not the case. To be sure, adrenalin production is arousing and can be scary for a brief period of time. Relax and let the natural course of arousal take its time. The first major drop in adrenaline takes 90 seconds. Thereafter, the body anxiety comes under control over the next 15–30 minutes.

During the 90 seconds, one is to engage in slow, deep breathing, muscle relaxation, visual imagery of some relaxing scene, or visualizing and saying five relaxing words repeatedly. Self-control is the ultimate objective for patients with anxiety and such emotional states.

Additional reading: Taylor, JB., *Whole Brain Living.*, Hat House Inc., 2022.

BE FAIR TO YOURSELF

Don't compare yourself with other people. Compare yourself to who you were yesterday.

Jordan B. Petersen

Who said it? Dr. Petersen (1962–) is a Canadian psychologist of considerable notoriety. He no longer maintains a clinical practice but focuses his attention on lecturing internationally. He is a superb lecturer. He has taught at the University of Toronto. In the process of his teaching and lecturing, audiences are educated in self-development and personal enhancement. He also has a large following of listeners for his daily podcasts and YouTube presentations. Radio and TV talk-show hosts also regularly interview him.

His primary book on the 12 Rules of Life is his attempt to address the chaos in our lives and how to prevent living lives of quiet desperation. Being responsible is the way to avoid suffering and live better.

This quote of his is meaningful considering the overriding message of Dr. Petersen. We all compare ourselves; however, most of the time we compare ourselves to other people, others who are better than us, better looking than us, or smarter than us. Comparison, then, is an exercise in futility. It is important that we identify ourselves as we are today, improve ourselves tomorrow, work to be the person we are, and live life fully.

We live in a world in which we compare ourselves to others based on our intelligence, appearance, productivity, and accomplishments. Unfortunately, we always see ourselves from the downside position, in which others are always better-looking, smarter, more accomplished, more productive, and so on. It's a no-win situation. It is better to be a stronger person tomorrow and then a better person the next day. The primary answer is in flipping the question around and comparing our life patterns with one another one day at a time. That is how one's personal values shine.

As Petersen is so outspoken and has opposed the political agenda of the government, he is often the subject of attack by the press and the current ruling liberal government in Canada. Even the current oversight committee of the psychology licensing body has attacked him. Attempts to get his license to practice as a psychologist have been relentless.

Additional reading: Petersen, J., *Life's 12 Lessons,* Random House Canada, 2018.

TOGETHER WE CAN DO IT

The most powerful force ever known on this planet is human cooperation—a force for construction and destruction.

Jonathan Haidt

Who said it? Dr. Haidt (1963–2018) is a social psychologist on the faculty of New York University's Stern School of Business. His areas of study relate to the psychology of morality. He has studied, to some extent, moral emotions and moral reasoning. He is well known for his four foundations of morality. His four foundational keys to morality are moral disgust, moral evaluation, social intuitionism, and moral foundations. His primary contributions span the last decade of the 1900s and the early 2000s. He is considered the "top global thinker" by Prospect magazine.

Dr. Haidt holds the view that human cooperation is one of the primary traits of interpersonal communication, relationships, and emotional experiences between two or more people. When cooperation prevails, a natural force is created, which results in constructive endeavors and achievements. However, he says that the same level of human cooperation can be a force of destruction when the cooperative dyad or triad has evil, immoral, or conflict-based motivation and intent.

Cooperation can result in a high level of construction, achievement, and accomplishment, but it can also result in severe degradation, deterioration, and destruction of relationships and communities. It is important that we choose constructive outcomes as we pursue human cooperation with others.

He has great concern for the changing culture on college campuses and its effects on mental health. We need more stories of moral beauty, as we are better for it. We need to talk about moral beauty and moral living. We need to promote morality at all levels of the community, especially among our youth.

Since 2018, Jonathan Haidt has studied the contributions of social media to the decline of teenage mental health and the rise of political dysfunction. He is unique in that he constructed a mission statement to conduct research on moral psychology and use those findings to help people understand each other and help important institutions work together.

He is currently a social psychologist at New York University's Stern School of Business. He studies the intuitive foundations of morality and how morality varies across cultures, including the cultures of progressive conservatives and libertarians. His goal is to help people understand each other, live and work near each other, and even learn from each other despite their moral differences.

His books include *The Happiness Hypothesis: Finding Modern Truth in Ancient Wisdom and The Coddling of the American Mind.* Both are excellent readings in the study of American youth today.

Additional reading: Heidt, J., *The Righteous Mind,* Knopf, 2013.

ONE GREAT TRAIT TO POSSSESS

Compassion does not render people tearful idlers, moral weaklings, or passive onlookers. But individuals of strength who will take on the pain of others, even when given the chance to skip out on such difficult actions or in anonymous conditions.

Dacher Keltner

Who said it? Dr. Keltner (1967–) was a key observer of emotional states and placed great emphasis in his research on the positive states of compassion, caring, empathy, and sympathy. He has found compassion to be the key and most powerful trait of all interpersonal traits.

Compassion was viewed as a key quality of all the interpersonal traits. Many times, we look upon people who are compassionate as actually being weak or overrun by emotion. Actually, compassion is a high quality. It is a behavior pattern that is learned and to be desired. We learn it from childhood. We learn it from our parents at home. We learn it from our peers and social contacts throughout life.

Throughout life, we are also given opportunities to be compassionate toward others. Either we act favorably and supportively, or we skip out on our responsibility and opportunity to be caring and healing in the life of someone else. We need to commit to a life based on compassion and enrich others and the world accordingly.

Parents need to make the trait of compassion a key focus and emphasis in their child-rearing practices with their children. Compassionate parents rear compassionate children who become compassionate adults.

Additional reading: Keltner, D., *The Main Source of Everyday Work and How It Can Transform Your Life*, Penquin Press, 2023.

LIVE WITH OPENNESS AND RECEPTIVITY

When we are open to new possibilities, we find them. Be open and skeptical of everything.

Todd Kashdan

Who said it? Todd Kashdan (1970–2018) is a researcher and speaker on motivational topics. He is an active and involved father of twins. His psychological practice focuses on and involves the reasons people suffer and are chronically anxious. He emphasized the meaning and purpose of life. His primary work took place during the early 2000s. He is a leading expert on the psychology of well-being, curiosity, mental flexibility, and social relationships. His book, The Upside of Your Dark Side, has been recognized widely. He also wrote the popular book, *The Art of Insubordination: How to Descend and Defy Effectively.*

Dr. Kashdan takes the position that positive emotions alone are not enough. Anger makes us creative; selflessness makes us brave; and guilt makes us motivated. The real key to success lies in emotional agility.

He holds the position that the greatest opportunity for joy, purpose, and personal growth does not, in fact, happen when we're searching for happiness. However, they are more likely to happen when we are mindful, when we explore what's novel, when we live in the moment, when we are open to new experiences, and when we relish the unknown. According to Kashdan, we are each to become curious explorers, comfortable with taking risks and challenges, and capable of functioning optimally in an unstable, unpredictable world.

Kashdan is currently employed as Director of the Well-Being Laboratory at George Mason University. There, he explores why people suffer from normal and pathological anxiety. He is also an authority on flexibility, well-being, curiosity, and resilience.

Dr. Kashdan focused his studies on possibility thinking, gratitude, and motivation. His primary message is for us to have an openness to new possibilities and look for them. If we look for them, we will find them. We need to be open, but we also need to be moderately skeptical at the same time.

He states, "Skepticism promotes questioning and the pursuit of knowledge and facts." Skepticism leads us in new directions and opens the door to new opportunities for thought, achievement, and lifestyle. Skepticism is the first and most basic component of scientific pursuit. Therefore, advancement in scientific understanding depends on healthy and honest skepticism.

He held the position that we cannot be open to the future and the possibilities of the future unless we live with a low level of fear and anxiety. In contrast, prominent levels of fear and anxiety close us down, limit our vision, and minimize our expectations and possibility thinking. Anyone who finds themselves being skeptical, doubtful, and fearful needs to resolve such basic emotions first so that possibility thinking becomes a reality and a possibility. We want to become open to everything while at the same time being skeptical about everything. It is the extremes to be avoided. Cautious openness is the key.

Additional reading: Kashdan, T., *The Art of Insubordination: How to Dissent and Defy Effectively.*, Avery Press, 2022.

EVEN FALSEHOODS CAN BE BELIEVED

A reliable way to make people believe in falsehoods is through frequent repetition, because familiarity is not easily distinguished from truth. Authoritarian institutions and marketers have always known this fact.

Daniel Kahneman

Who said it? Kahneman (1975–) was a psychologist, a Harvard professor, the winner of the Nobel Prize in Economics, and also the recipient of the Presidential Medal of Freedom. He studied judgment and decision-making and conducted experiments involving loss of version. He explains that memories can play a trick on our minds when remembering experiences and how to avoid bias in the corporate hiring process. He recounts his childhood growing up in Nazi-occupied France and his encounter with an SS soldier. He breaks down decision-making hygiene and how it relates to vaccines. He is the host of the podcast, *Under the Cortex*.

He contends that because we are subject to hidden influences when making judgments and decisions, we cannot be internally consistent. He considers the human mind to function in two systems. System one is the fast process that operates automatically and usually outside our awareness. It served as an unconscious mind.

System two is when we operate on input that is more demanding or when effortful self-control is required. It is System 2 that gets the last word. System 2 serves like a conscious or thinking mind.

He states that changing one's mind about human nature is challenging work, and changing one's mind for the worse about oneself is even harder. The best way to understand the two systems is to recognize the signs that you are in a "cognitive mind field." Slow down and ask for reinforcement from System 2. However, and unfortunately, system two is often sluggish in coming to our aid. Illusions and biases in our thinking are hard to recognize. As a result, we fail to exercise caution when we need it most.

As a Harvard professor, he focused his research on the area of social and political thought patterns, how they develop, and how they influence our lives.

Particularly in the political arena, it is commonly understood that any identified event or interpretation of an event, if frequently repeated so that people will remember the statement and think of it as being true, whether it is or not, becomes a fact. This soon became a strategy in politics and marketing. To be sure, a particular point of view was repeatedly stated in diverse ways, in different situations, and by different people, all assuring that the statement would in fact be accepted as true even when it was not. Certainly, this concept raises the question of ethics, morality, and honesty in the media and advertising marketplaces of life.

Accordingly, Kahneman advocated for the idea, "What you see is all there is." He gave much thought to the idea of why we see something and not other things. He concluded that our hyper-focus at the time compared to making a casual observation was the reason.

Additional reading: Kahneman, D., *Thinking fast and slow*, Farrar, Straus, and Giroux, 2011.

A SUPPORT SYSTEM IN NECESSARY

When we encounter an unexpected challenge or threat, the only way to save ourselves is to hold on tight to the people around us and not let go.

Shawn Achor

Who is it? Dr. Achor (1978–) is an interpersonal social psychologist. His research is designed to help us understand the role of support systems in our lives, especially at times of challenge and unusual stress.

Dr. Achor's quote is a strong reminder that challenges and threats happen to all of us, often unexpectedly. It is therefore important that we have a support system in place so that when a challenge or threat comes our way, we have support people to go to and be around. We are not to let go of them until we are able to resolve that threat and move forward in life. It is important that we not hold on too long and become dependent, however.

Threats, trauma, and elevated levels of stress can bring us into the lives of other people or cause us to isolate, which is unacceptable, inappropriate, and potentially destructive. It is the pre-selected support people who are around when we are challenged. People who have gone through the same challenges or who are going through the same challenges are usually preferred as our support persons of choice.

To be sure, misery loves company, but it is best to have people who have gone through that same misery or who are going through that same misery at the same time as you. It is essential to understand each other and be bonded so we can more firmly and in a healthy manner hold onto one another until the storm passes by. During a trauma or crisis, it is not the time to find a support system or person. Support systems need to be in place well in advance of any trauma that might come along. As it has been said, "It is no time to learn to swim when the rainstorm hits."

Additional reading: Achor, S., *The Happiness Advantage*, 2018.

YOU CAN DO IT

Every person on this earth is full of great possibilities that can be realized through imagination, effort, and perseverance.

Scott Barry Kaufmann

Who said it? Dr. Kaufmann (1979–) is a professor of psychology at Colombia University, focusing on the cognitive and human potential for creativity and the development of the mind. His research is used to help us live fully, creatively, and productively. He is an active professional pursuing his research and writing passion while teaching.

To be sure, we all have within us the possibility of greatness, achievement, and success. However, it does not come easily. It comes with a price. The price is effort—day-to-day effort. It means perseverance to go on and on, perseverance to the end, and seeing the conclusion of a project and its ultimate contribution to society. was Yale-educated. He was of the basic belief that creativity and imagination can change the world for the better. He spoke on topics such as achieving greatness and the development of intelligence, creativity, and personality. His book, *TRANSEND: The New Science of Self-Actualization, helps put this issue in perspective.*

For Dr. Kaufman, it all starts with imagination. He encourages us to imagine what we would like to accomplish. Then focus on what we can accomplish. Imagine what we could accomplish and what the world would be like if society and other people adopted our accomplishments as part of their lifestyles. We need to commit to achieving growth and pursue self-actualization each day. Our trauma leads us in the pursuit of personal growth, identity, and purpose. There are all kinds of bright minds. Our personal goal is to navigate the choppy waters of everyday living and work to achieve self-actualization.

Additional reading: Kaufmann, S.B., *Choose Growth*, TarcherPerigee, 2023.

THE POWER OF CULTURE

There's been a big expansion in our culture of what we view as harmful, and that affects how we respond to things; it even affects our anxiety levels.

Payton Jones

Who said it? Dr. Jones (1995) points out that even though the rate of violence has decreased over time, the rate of post-trauma stress disorders has remained constant. Her studies helped us define trauma and what must be included to make up a stressful and traumatic event.

It is easy to become immune to stress and various harmful events. Unfortunately, when such events become commonplace and seen as some type of regular occurring event in life, we relax and lower our guard. That may not be good, however. We may be caught off guard and vulnerable.

There is a mid-point. It is wise to be on guard, but we need to keep it moderate and reasonable. Moderate levels of anxiety are better than elevated levels of anxiety at any time. Our response to any situation needs to be measured and not histrionic. Being prepared is always the best posture. One cannot assume things are under control when they are not.

One more thing. We may be using the diagnosis of post-traumatic stress disorder more freely these days. It may seem like there is more trauma, but it is unrelated to violence. Hence, it is a spurious correlation. They are unrelated. We need to address the two issues separately.

The irony is that she studied trauma; she died from trauma—a tragic automobile accident. She left behind a significant trail of influence in the lives of many teenagers and children A premature death ended a career that was in the making.

Additional reading: Jones, Payton, *What's in a Trauma: Using Machine Learning to Unpack What Makes an Even More Traumatic*. Journal of Affective Disorders., 2021.

MAY NOT BE TRUE OR HELPFUL

We have this nugget of wisdom that warnings are always good; to be forewarned is to be forearmed.

Victoria Bridgeland

Who is it? Dr. Bridgeland (1996–) of Australia's Flinders University has studied considerably the role of trigger warnings. When something is coming and thought to be potentially upsetting, discomforting, or hurtful to a particular person, warning signs are sent out so people can prepare accordingly. Forewarning and trigger warnings have become popular and thought to be helpful as we have increasingly focused on and tried to prevent potential trauma and stressful events.

Unfortunately, the research in the area of trigger warnings has been surprising. It does not help people prepare for a difficult situation, and it does not harm people intended to be helped. Generally speaking, trigger warnings make people feel more anxious about the material event in question by encouraging them to see trauma as more central and quite powerful to their life narrative.

Even the converse is true. The more people identify as trauma victims and ask for accommodations, such as in the classroom or work environment, such efforts can reinforce their sense of victimhood or potential to be victims. Using trigger warnings is often a well-meaning effort, but the intention to make people more comfortable does not always play out the way we expect it to.

Forewarnings often make us, as the sender of the warning, feel better, even if it does not help prepare someone for a coming event. While it may make sense to forewarn people of a coming trauma, it helps the sender more than the receiver of such a message. The actual role of forewarnings is yet to be fully understood.

She also investigated emotional regulation, expectancy effects, and memory for traumatic events.

Additional reading: Bridgeland, Victoria. *A Meta-Analysis of the Effects of Trigger Warnings, Content Warning, and Content Notes*, 2022.

ADDITIONAL WORDS OF WISDOM FOR OUR CONSIDERATION

THERAUPTIC OUTCOME

The therapeutic alliance based on trust, compatibility, and likability between a patient and therapist is one of the best predictors of psychotherapy and medical-surgical outcomes.

Tori DeAngelis

Who said it? Trust, compatibility, and likeability have become well regarded in the psychological and medical practice professions and strongly influence outcomes. Patients are advised to seek out a professional provider according to these critical relationship factors. Tori DeAngelis (1980–) has been a strong advocate for the professional and the patient, forming a strong alliance based on trust and likeability from the very beginning of their relationship.

While she is not a psychologist herself, she might as well be, as she has written, as a journalist, hundreds of articles on psychological topics for the public and the psychological community.

For instance, she claimed that the doctor-patient relationship affects the outcomes of psychotherapy and major medical procedures. Allowing someone to impact your life in significant ways requires the act of submission. Submission, for example, requires trust and confidence in the person you will allow to influence you or perform major medical procedures on you. Patients need to know their doctor and take time to consider these important relationship factors before agreeing to proceed with a course of therapy or any medical procedures. Likewise, doctors need to allow time and opportunity for a trusting relationship to be established. An alliance between the professional and the patient is not friendship but a well-defined relationship based on trust, likeability, and compatibility. Confidence results. A better outcome is more likely to result. Remember, it is a team effort, always.

Tori has written hundreds of articles on various topics of psychology, essentially taking the research findings of a psychologist and putting the findings into the language of the common reader. The field of psychology needs more writers like Tori. We need help in getting the word out.

Additional reading: DeAngelis, T., *Want to boost your mental health? Take a walk.* Monitor on Psychology, 2022.

THE FOUNDATIONAL STONE OF THRIVING

Keep the faith to the utmost.

Anonymous

Who said it? While unknown, the quote implies that the professional who spoke such words was to have been a person of faith, realized the importance of faith, and urged that faith play a role in the lives of patients. Faith has become increasingly recognized as a critical component of a person's mental health, especially since the onset of positive psychology. The two components are mutually important. Have faith and keep it under all circumstances. One's faith is to be advanced and viewed as alive and well.

Faith begets hope, and it is the hope we have that generates positive living and expectations. A mentally healthy individual lives with hope based on the associated component of faith. We live better each day as we have a future in mind and anticipate that future with positive expectations based on one's personal faith.

Faith and hope are basic to human stability and the ability to thrive. It has always been the case. It is true today as well.

Additional reading: Hood, B., *The Psychology of Religion*, The Guilford Press, 2018.

THE OTHERS IN YOUR LIFE

Make as many friends as possible, and never forget that your success depends on others.

Author Unknown

Who said it? While the author is unknown, it was obviously a therapist who empathizes with people in their emptiness and loneliness. Therapists can be as cold and unfeeling as anyone else. Perhaps even display tough love at times. What patients need are mentoring and supportive relationships that foster warmth and compassion. Several such mentors are better than one.

Empathy is a major quality of an effective therapist as well as of highly functioning people. Relationships are built on the ability to identify with and bond with others. Empathy is the key factor in bringing two people together to experience mutual happiness, intimacy, and mutual achievement.

By all means. We function within the framework of quality and dependable friends. It is important that we, as therapists, be such people and that we help others develop such traits as well. Certainly, we are to foster such warmth in all our relationships. Those are the relationships that flourish over time.

Additional reading: Moojani, A., *Sensitive is the New Strong: The Power of Epaths in an Increasingly Harsh World,* Atria/Enliven Books, 2021.

APPENDIX

HISTORY OF THE AMERICAN PSYCHOLOGICAL ASSSOCCIATION (APA)

The American Psychological Association was founded in 1892 with thirty-one members and grew quickly after World War II. Today, APA is the largest scientific and professional organization representing psychology in the United States, with more than 121,000 researchers, educators, clinicians, consultants, and students as its members. APA also has fifty-four divisions representing the subfields of psychology.

The Founding of APA

APA was founded in July 1892 by a small group of men interested in what they called "the new psychology." The group elected 31 individuals, including themselves, to membership, with **G. Stanley Hall** as its first president.

1. of the APA consisted of a council with an executive committee. This structure continued to the beginning of the twenty-first century. APA's founding was part of a large number of changes occurring in the United States at that time, including:
2. The **emergence of academic disciplines** such as psychology, economics, political science, biochemistry, and physiology. These new disciplines quickly developed advanced degrees that provided credentials to validate the disciplines' members as experts.
3. The **progressive movement in politics** called for a more efficient, less corrupt social order.

4. The constructive interaction of these two developments—specialized expertise and rationalized government—helped create the need for trained personnel to fill the new professional niches created by the demands for a more efficient society. The first meeting was held in December 1892 at the University of Pennsylvania. Realizing that the growth of applied psychology represented a potential threat to its preeminence, the leaders of the APA reorganized during World War II. The association's new scope included professional practice and the promotion of human welfare, as well as the practice of the science of psychology. This flexibility in scope has remained to the present.

The Effects of WWI and WWII

Psychology boomed after the end of World War II, with the greatest increase in membership coming between 1940 and 1970. Several factors fueled this growth:

- Many **returning service members** saw the great need for better psychological services firsthand during the war.
- **The GI Bill,** the new Veterans Administration Clinical Psychology training program, and the creation of the **National Institute of Mental Health** contributed to the increased interest in psychology.
- For the first time, psychology was a field, in both science and practice, that was richly funded for training and research.

Over the years, APA has grown in membership and has been a voice of influence on various social and scientific issues that have emerged and challenged us as a society.

American Psychology Association, 2008

FORMER APA PRESIDENTS

2024 Cynthia de las Fuentes

2023 Thema S. Bryant

2022 Frank C. Worrell

2021 Jennifer F. Kelly, PhD, ABPP

2020 Sandra L. Shullman, PhD

2019 Rosie Phillips Davis, PhD, ABPP

2018 Jessica Henderson Daniel, PhD, ABPP

2017 Antonio E. Puente, PhD

2016 Susan H. McDaniel, PhD

2015 Barry S. Anton, PhD, ABPP

2014 Nadine J. Kaslow, PhD, ABPP

2013 Donald N. Bersoff, PhD, JD

2012 Suzanne Bennett Johnson, PhD

2011 Melba J.T. Vasquez, PhD

2010 Carol D. Goodheart, EdD

2009 James H. Bray, PhD

2008 Alan E. Kazdin, PhD

2007 Sharon Stephens Brehm, PhD

2006 Gerald P. Koocher, PhD

2005 Ronald F. Levant, EdD, ABPP

2004 Diane F. Halpern, PhD

2003 R obert J. Sternberg, PhD

2002 Philip G. Zimbardo, PhD

2001 Norine G. Johnson, PhD

2000 Patrick H. Deleon, PhD, MPH, JD

1999 Richard M. Suinn, PhD

1998 Martin E.P. Seligman, PhD

1997 Norman Abeles, PhD

1996 Dorothy W. Cantor, PsyD

1995 Robert J. Resnick, PhD, ABPP

1994 Ronald E. Fox, PhD

1993 Frank Farley, PhD

1992 Jack Wiggins, Jr., PhD

1991 Charles Spielberger, PhD

1990 Stanley Graham, PhD

1989 Joseph D. Matarazzo, PhD

1988 Raymond D. Fowler, PhD

1987 Bonnie R. Strickland, PhD

1986 Logan Wright, PhD

1985 Robert Perloff, PhD

1984 Janet T. Spence, PhD

1983 Max Siegal, PhD

1982 William Bevan, PhD

1981 John J. Conger, PhD

1980 Florence L. Denmark, PhD

1979 Nicholas A. Cummings, PhD

1978 M. Brewster Smith, PhD

1977 Theodore Blau, PhD

1976 Wilbert J. Mckeachie, PhD

1975 Donald T. Campbell, PhD

1974 Albert Bandura, PhD

1973 Leona E. Tyler, PhD

1972 Anne Anastasi, PhD

1971 Kenneth B. Clark, PhD

1970 George W. Albee, PhD

1969 George A. Miller, PhD

1968 A. H. Maslow, PhD

1967 Gardner Lindzey, PhD

1966 Nicholas Hobbs, PhD

1965 Jerome Bruner, PhD

1964 Quinn McNemar, PhD

1963 Charles E. Osgood, PhD

1962 Paul E. Meehl, PhD

1961 Neal E. Miller, PhD

1960 Donald O. Hebb, PhD

1959 W. Kohler, PhD

1958 H. F. Harlow, PhD

1957 Lee J. Cronbach, PhD

1956 Theodore M. Newcomb, PhD

1955 E. Lowell Kelly, PhD

1954 O. H. Mowrer, PhD

1953 Laurence Frederic Shaffer, PhD

1952 Joseph McVicker Hunt, PhD

1951 Robert R. Sears, PhD

1950 Joy Paul Guilford, PhD

1949 Ernest R. Hilgard, PhD

1948 Donald G. Marquls, PhD

1947 Carl R. Rogers, PhD

1946 Henry E. Garrett, PhD

1945 Edwin R. Guthrie, PhD

1944 Gardner Murphy, PhD

1943 John Edward Anderson, PhD

1942 Calvin Perry Stone, PhD

1941 Herbert Woodrow, PhD

1940 Leonard Carmichael, PhD

1939 Gordon Willard Allport, PhD

1938 John Frederick Dashiell, PhD

1937 Edward Chace Tolman, PhD

1936 Clark Leonard Hull, PhD

1935 Albert Theodore Poffenberger, PhD

1934 Joseph Peterson, PhD

1933 Louis Leon Thurstone, PhD

1932 Walter Richard Miles, PhD

1931 Walther Samuel Hunter, PhD

1930 Herbert Sidney Langfeld, PhD

1929 Karl Lashley, PhD

1928 Edwin Garrigues Boring, PhD

1927 Harry Levi Hollingsworth, PhD

1926 Harvey A. Carr, PhD

1925 Madison Bentley, PhD

1924 Granville Stanley Hall, PhD

1923 Lewis Madison Terman, PhD

1922 Knight Dunlap, PhD

1921 Margaret Floy Washburn, PhD

1920 Shepard Ivory Franz, PhD

1919 Walter Dill Scott, PhD

1918 John Wallace Baird, PhD

1917 Robert Mearns Yerkes, PhD

1916 Raymond Dodge, PhD

1915 John Broadus Watson, PhD

1914 Robert Sessions Woodworth, PhD

1913 Howard Crosby Warren, PhD

1912 Edward Lee Thorndike, PhD

1911 Carl Emil Seashore, PhD

1910 Walter Bowers Pillsbury, PhD

1909 Charles Hubbard Judd, PhD

1908 George Malcolm Stratton, PhD

1907 Henry Rutgers Marshall, AM

1906 James Rowland Angell, MA

1905 Mary Whiton Calkins, AM

1904 William James, MD

1903 William Lowe Bryan, PhD

1902 Edmund Clark Sanford, PhD

1901 Josiah Royce, PhD

1900 Joseph Jastrow, PhD

1899 John Dewey, PhD

1898 Hugo Munsterberg, PhD

1897 James Mark Baldwin, PhD

1896 George Stuart Fullerton, MA

1895 James McKeen Cattell, PhD

1894 William James, MD

1893 George Trumbull Ladd, PhD

1892 Granville Stanley Hall, PhD

NOTED PSYCHOLOGISTS OF RECOGNITION

Hippocrates – The Father of Medicine

Wilheim Wundt – The Father of Psychology

William James: The Father of American Psychology

Franz Gall: The Skull Reader

James Cattell: The Professor of Psychology

Sigmund Freud: The Father of Psychotherapy

The sample of children on which the famous intelligence test was based: Terman's Termites

Lev Vygotsky: The Mozart of Psychology

Edward Titchener: The Professor

Ellan Langer: The Mother of Mindfulness

Mary Cover Jones: The Mother of Behavior Therapy

Kurt Lewin: The Father of Social Psychology

Don Mac Mannis: Dr. Mac: The Singing Psychologist

HISTORY OF PSYCHOLOGY AT THE STATE LEVEL

The early history of clinical psychology training at the state level emerged in the latter part of the 1800s. For example, in the state of California, psychological training emerged with the founding of Leeland Stanford Junior University in 1885 and the recruitment of Frank Angell, a student of Wilhelm Wundt, to lead Stanford's new psychology department.

The separation of psychology as a specialty and free-standing departments of scientific study from its pre-existing place within the Department of Philosophy to become its own freestanding department further marked the evolution of psychological training. This took place in the early 1920s.

This process was repeated in many states with the establishment of two areas of study, the Department of Philosophy and the Department of Psychology, and the associated doctorate degrees issued by these departments. As a result, psychology became an increasingly independent and vigorous scientific area of study.

At the same time, small Ph.D. programs from major research institutions offered the vast majority of doctorate-level psychological training, which diminished the clinical training components in favor of a stronger research focus. The demand for psychologists within the states to teach and provide counseling services began to far exceed the number of psychologists graduating from the various universities. Major research institutions frequently reduced or eliminated psychology training programs in favor of experimental psychological studies, which exacerbated the demand. Many professionals within the field began advocating for a major change in the format for training clinicians nationwide. Clinical science became de-emphasized, and clinical training was given more attention and development. Clinical training within the academic universities diminished, and a re-focusing took place, separating psychologists of clinical science from psychology as an applied science.

This eventually led in the early 1970's to the formation of Psy.D. clinical training throughout the country, starting with the University of Illinois, and then Baylor University followed shortly thereafter.

From there, it spread across the nation, with most schools offering the Ph.D. degree based on experimental psychology and the Psy.D. degree based on applied psychological research.

TRENDS IN THE STUDY OF PSYCHOLOGY

The Changing Focus From 1895 Through 2024:

- Quantitative: The pursuit of measuring and quantifying a particular stimulus or experience, such as a "just-notable difference" for sounds or images.
- Qualitative: The exploration of the person and what makes up the essence of one person over another, such as personality traits.
- Neurological: The scientific study of the brain and its functions in organizing the behavior patterns of man.
- Applied: The study of the characteristics of a person and how such traits and abilities can be used to place men in occupations of value and compatibility.
- Clinical: The study and practice of abnormal behavior and thinking patterns as well as how to correct such patterns for the good of the patient and society.
- Popularization: The paradigm shifts in applying psychological research funding for popular daily living effectiveness.

The Nine Schools of Psychology and Their Primary Advocates:

STRUCTURALISM. . . Wundt

FUNCTIONALISM. . . James

PSYCHOANALYTIC THEORY. . . Freud

GESTALT PSYCHOLOGY. . . Wertheimer, Koffka, Kohler

BEHAVIORISM. . . Pavlov, Watson, Skinner

HUMANISM. . . Maslow, Rogers

COGNITIVE REVOLUTION. . . Chomsky, Miller, Weisstein, Crawford, and Marecek

MUTICULTURAL PSYCHOLOGY. . . Summer, Black, and Franko

MEDICAL PSYCHIATRY IS BORN

In October of 1844, a group of thirteen physicians met together at the Jones Hotel in Philadelphia to form the Association of Medical Superintendents of American Institutions for the Insane. The association eventually became the American Psychiatric Association. This preceded, for three years, the establishment of the American Medical Association. It was then superseded by the American Medical Psychological Association in 1892, which continued until 1919.

The thirteen delegates attending the meeting were physician superintendents, representing thirteen of the thirty-one asylums and hospitals available for the care of insane people. The purpose of establishing the association was "to secure for the future a higher standard for hospitals and more liberal and enlightened treatment for all sufferers from mental diseases."

The thirteen superintendents meeting on that day were the following:

- Amariah Brigham
- William M. Awl
- Pliny Earic
- Samuel B. Woodward*
- Charles H. Stedman
- Francis T. Stribling
- Nehemiah Cutter
- Luther V. Bell
- James S. Beller
- Samuel White*
- Thomas S. Kirkbride*
- Isaac Ray
- John M. Gatt

Together, they elected Samuel B. Woodward to be president, Samuel White to be vice president, and Thomas S. Kirkbride to be secretary/treasurer. This association of medical superintendents continued to meet as a formal body from 1844 to 1889. They formed 16 different committees, representing a wide-ranging concern in the area of patient care.

The topics for consideration included the following:

- Moral Treatment of Insanity
- Restraint and Restraining Apparatus
- Construction of Hospitals for the Insane
- Statistics of Insanity
- Jurisprudence of Insanity
- Prevention of Suicide
- Support of the Pauper Insane
- Proper Provisions for Insane Prisoners
- Post-Mortem Examinations
- Causes and Preventions of Insanity

These 13 men were known for their energy, industry, and talent. They contributed not only to the founding of the American Psychiatric Association and its early development, but also to the embryonic field of psychiatry, in which areas of jurisprudence, construction of hospitals, hospital statistics, problems of alcoholism, and the definition of early therapies were issues of concern and strategic planning.

The philosophy of care espoused was one of enlightened humanitarianism. This was markedly different than what had been the case previously. Previously, patients experienced much misunderstanding, stigmatization, and cruel treatment.

THE FIRST THREE PSYCHIATRIC HOSPITALS IN THE USA

- Eastern State Hospital, Virginia, Dr. John Galt, Superintendent, 1844
- Western State Hospital, Virginia, Dr. Francis Stribling, Superintendent, 1844
- Central Lunatic Asylum for Colored Insane, Dr. Olivia Garland, Superintendent, Virginia, 1870

(Bernstein, Dorothy, American Journal of Psychiatry, 151:1, January 1994).

TWELVE CHARACTERISTICS COMMON TO HISTORICALLY FAMOUS THERAPISTS

Based on a review of the similarities among the therapists included in this volume, the following twelve factors were identified as being fairly common among them:

- PROLIFIC PUBLISHED AUTHORS
- RESOLUTE PROFESSORS
- SYSTEMATIC RESEARCHERS
- INTENSLEY FOCUSED ON A SUBJECT OF INTEREST AND PASSION
- ACTIVE IN ADVANCING THE PROFESSION OF PSYCHOLOGY
- HONORED BY COLLEAGUES
- ENCOURAGED MENTOREES
- ASSOCIATED WITH MAJOR UNIVERSITIES AND INSTITUTES OF LEARNING
- WIDELY KNOWN FOR A SPECIFIC AREA OF STUDY
- CREATE A LIST OF STUDENTS WHO CONTINUED THEIR THEORIES AND RESEARCH AFTER THEY DIED OR RETIRED.
- OFTEN INVOLVED IN CONTROVERSY
- KEPT A RESPECTFUL DISTANCE FROM THEIR STUDENTS AND PATIENTS
- MANY PEOPLE STUDIED PSYCHOLOGY AS A SECOND FIELD OF STUDY.

FAMOUS PAPERS IN THE HISTORY OF PSYCHOLOGY

- I'M OK, YOU'RE OK
- THE NATURE OF PREJUDICE
- LITTLE ALBERT
- A GUIDE TO RATIONAL LIVING
- THE FEMALE BRAIN
- THE BLANK SLATE
- THE MARSHMALLOW TEST
- THE INTERPRETATION OF DREAMS
- WORKING WITH EMOTIONAL INELLIGENCE
- BEYOND FREEDOM AND DIGNITY
- GAMES PEOPLE PLAY
- THE MAN WHO MISTOOK HIS WIFE FOR A HAT
- ON BECOMING A PERSON
- AUTHENTIC HAPPINESS
- ON BECOMING A PERSON
- THE WILL TO MEANING
- THE TRUE BELIEVER
- MY VOICE WILL GO WITH YOU
- THE EXAMINED LIFE
- OUR INNER CONFLICTS
- THE SEVEN PRINCIPLES OF MAKING MARRIAGE WORK
- LIFE'S 12 LESSONS
- THE DENIAL OF DEATH
- THE BELL JAR
- THE SEASONS OF A MAN'S LIFE

OTHER FAMOUS AND WORTHY PSYCHOLOGISTS

No book can completely cover the contributions and significance of every psychologist. In many ways, every psychologist contributes not only to their patients and their community, but even, in a broader sense, to society at large. Many benefit secondarily from the therapy sessions of others as the insights are passed along. For instance, a patient's family member may gain from the therapy that another family member received, or an office coworker may gain from the significant changes that occurred in another coworker's life as a result of the therapy that they both received.

Who are some of the additional famous psychologists that could have or should have been mentioned in this book and might be the basis for a sequel? Consider the following professionals and pursue their contributions as you have interest and time:

1. Stanley Schachter
2. Neil E. Miller
3. Edward Thorndike
4. David C. McClelland
5. Kurt Lewen
6. Clark L. Hull
7. Jerome Kagan
8. Jerome S. Bruner
9. Ernest R. Hilgard
10. Lawrence Kohlberg
11. Martin EP Seligman
12. Donald T. Campbell
13. Endel Tulving

14. Noam Chomsky
15. Suliman Asch
16. Stanley Milgram
17. George Kelley
18. Charles E. Osgood
19. Roger W. Sperry
20. Edward C. Tolman
21. Lee Cronbach
22. Wolfgang Kohler
23. David Wechsler
24. Leonard Berkowitz
25. Richard Lazarus
26. L. L. Thurston
27. Margaret Washburn
28. Orval Hobart Mowrer
29. Theodore Millon
30. Mihaly Csikszentmihalyi

The reader is encouraged to pursue their own interests and knowledge of historical figures in psychology and come to appreciate their place in the development of psychology over the centuries. There are many who have made a significant contribution but may not have been as public or as published as the men and women selected for this volume. Yes, the book could go on and on or have a sequel.

PERSONAL OPPORTUNITIES I HAVE HAD TO EXPANDMY KNOWLEDGE AND EXPERIENCE FROM THESEFAMOUS PSYCHOLOGISTS

- I visited the research laboratory of Harry Harlow to view his research with monkeys. I recall how the monkeys immediately ran to the cloth mother as I walked into the room, creating a level of fear for them. (1962)
- I had the privilege of being taught the testing of intelligence by one of the "Terman Termites." He told us the story of how he was selected for the task and how he was repeatedly evaluated over time to assess his intelligence. Indeed, he was a very bright man. Dr. Bishoff was his name. (1962)
- I recall my visit to the University of Chicago to hear Victor Frankl personally deliver a speech on his war and concentration camp experiences. (1963).
- My visit to the University of Lund's library and a personal tour of the inner archives to view the original handwritten documents of the early 1700–1800s Swedish psychology scholars were very impactful. (1964)
- I recall my personal conversation with Dr. Muzafer Sherif, in which he invited me to come to Oklahoma State University to study for the Ph.D. degree with him as his research assistant. (1964) I declined the invitation, however.
- My visit to the Montreal Neurological Research Laboratory, where many great brain researchers have studied the brain over the years, was very stimulating. (1968)
- It was my personal privilege to study on two separate occasions for a month each time under the teaching of Dr. Wolpe at

the Eastern Pennsylvania Psychiatric Institute and learn the use of progressive relaxation to treat anxiety and other anxiety-based disorders. (1968 and 1970)

- It was also my privilege to study for three months under the direction of Dr. Ernest Poser of Montreal, Quebec, Canada. Dr. Poser was one of Canada's foremost behavior therapists. I studied and worked as a graduate intern implementing behavior therapy methods on a calcitrant adult psychiatric population at the Verdun Provincial Hospital. (1969)
- It was my privilege to be involved in the development of the Psy.D. degree in psychology at Baylor University, the second graduate school to develop and offer the Psy.D. degree in clinical psychology. (1971 -73)
- I recall a personal audience with the psychiatrist and former student of Anna Freud, Dr. Elsie Colette. She proved to be a delightful professional and offered a stimulating discussion during our two-hour talk over lunch. (1974)
- I was privileged to visit St. Paul's Cathedral in Geneva, Switzerland, where Paul Tournie's father served as a pastor and where Dr. Tournie and his family attended. John Calvin served as the pastor of the church some 200 years previously. (2017)
- I had the privilege of examining a young Ph.D. student of B. F. Skinner for licensing as a psychologist in the State of California. He was well trained.
- While I never had the privilege of meeting Dr. Eysenck of England, I did have as my professors five of his students who had immigrated to Canada and were on the faculty of Queen's University, where I obtained my Ph.D. degree. Likewise, I had not met Dr. Julian Rotter but was taught by three of his graduates at Northern Illinois University. . . All were first-generation Ph.D. students or professors.
- I had the privilege of teaching the graduates of Trinity Western University along with Drs. Paul Wong and Marvin McDonald.
- I had the privilege of sharing office space with Drs. Lindquist, Ohanesian, and Parker, all honorable and exemplary therapists and mentors.

SELECTED BOOKS BY HEDBERG

Psychotherapy Through a One-Way Window

Living Life @ its Best

Better Parenting

Out of the Darkness of Depression

Legacy: A Place to Park My Story

Jonathan Edwards: A Life Well Lived

Heroes in Blue

Lessons from My Father

Doctor, Teach Me to Parent

Achieving and Living a Healthy Lifestyle in a World of Stress

Kids Alive

Deep Roots

(All books are available through Amazon or your local book seller.)

MEDIA RESOURCES BY DR. HEDBERG

www.thepsychologyreport.buzzsprout.com

You Tube: Allan Hedberg

www.booksbyhedberg.com

The Psychology Report Blog

DISCLAIMER

First, let me admit that I am not a historian of psychological history. However, I am a clinical psychologist with a special interest in history. Hence, I wrote and compiled this book as a "recorder of history." This book is the outcome of my efforts to learn about our history and record it as one of the final acts of my professional career of over 50 years.

Historical psychologists and therapists were selected to be included in this volume. I have tried to capture the essence of psychology over time, its significant developments, and its contributions to our science and society. Obviously, many others could have been included. Society has benefited from every therapist and research psychologist around the globe throughout time. It would take many volumes to capture all the ways psychologists have contributed to an ever-more complex society.

In compiling this book," I stand on the shoulders" of many men and women who were selected for their valued contributions to the growth of psychology into a mature and valued profession. It is with sincere grace and discretion that only 100 dedicated professionals have been selected and honored. I leave it to the next historian of psychology to identify others and highlight their contributions and significance to the profession and the world.

Some of the therapists were consulted about their inclusion in this book. Others were not for various and obvious reasons. I trust I have represented each of them accurately and in a professional manner.

Finally, I thank those noted in my references for their background research, on which I drew heavily, and the studies they conducted to help me and all of us understand our history and appreciate all those who contributed to its maturity over the years. While others have written more extensively, I tried to keep my summary comments, based on the writings of many, on each professional in a "Readers Digest" manner.

One last point: Not only am I a recorder of history, but I am also a therapist who loves to refer to our history and educate patients on relevant points of our history as they apply to their particular situation. For example, a mother recently asked me why she and her daughter never bonded. It was a wonderful way to generate a constructive discussion on the topic and help her process the loss of her mother's dream. I based my discussion on the research of Bowlby and Harlow. It so happened that the daughter was born premature and spent the first year of her life in the hospital. Sadly, the mother was only able to visit on a predetermined schedule. Her experience was close to the research and findings of these two historical psychologists.

Enjoy the read. Increase your interest in our history.

SELECTED REFERENCES

Boring, E., This History of Experimental Psychology, Prentice-Hall, 1950.

Brainy Quotes, 2001–2023

Butler-Bowdon, T., 50 Psychology Classics, Nicholas Brealey, 2017.

Cherry, Kendra, Great-Psychology-Quotes, www.verywellmind.com, 2022

Diggins, John Patrick, The Rise and Fall of the American Left, W.W. Norton and Company, 1975.

Furumoto and Scarborough, *Placing Women in the History of Psychology,* American Psychologist, pp. 35–42, 1986.

Guthrie, R.V. (1998), Even the Rat Was White: A Historical View of Psychology. Boston: Allyn and Bacon.

Hunt, M., The Story of Psychology, Anchor Books, 1993.

Jacobus, L.E., A World of Ideas, Bedford/ST. Martins, 2010.

Swartz, K., and Pfister, R., *Perspective on Psychological Science,* Vol. 11., 2016, 399–407

Warren, Rebecca, Editor; The Psychology Book, Penguin Random House, New York, 2017

https//en.Wikipedia (searched by name of psychologist)

The blogs, podcasts, and web sites of many psychologists are included in the book.

The publisher's descriptions of the books written by the various psychologists included in this book.

Documents of the American Psychological Association, as identified in the book.

THE HISTORY OF PSYCHOLOGY:
The Contributions of 100 Historical Figures

Allan G. Hedberg, Ph.D.
Clinical Psychologist

QUOTABLE THERAPISTS FROM HISTORY

1. **Erich Fromm**: "Being entirely honest with oneself is a good exercise."
2. **Sigmund Freud**: "Out of your vulnerabilities will come your strength."
3. **Carl G. Jung**: "Everything that irritates us about others can lead us to an understanding of ourselves."
4. **Carl Rogers**: "When I look at the world, I am pessimistic, but when I look at other people, I am optimistic."
5. **B.F. Skinner**: "A failure is not always a mistake; it may simply be the best one can do under the circumstances."
6. **Philip Zimbardo**: "If you put good apples in a bad situation, you will get bad apples."
7. **Jordan Peterson**:" Don't compare yourself to others; compare yourself to who you were yesterday."

www.ingramcontent.com/pod-product-compliance
Lightning Source LLC
Chambersburg PA
CBHW052111030426
42335CB00025B/2935

* 9 7 9 8 8 9 4 6 5 0 3 0 2 *